# NOW
# I LAY ME DOWN
# TO SLEEP

# NOW
# I LAY ME DOWN
# TO SLEEP

Ron McGregor

| Library of Congress Control Number: | | 2013900982 |
|---|---|---|
| ISBN: | Hardcover | 978-1-4797-8098-3 |
| | Softcover | 978-1-4797-8097-6 |
| | Ebook | 978-1-4797-8099-0 |

This book was printed in the United States of America.

Rev. date: 04/10/13

**To order additional copies of this book, contact:**
Xlibris Corporation
1-888-795-4274
www.Xlibris.com
Orders@Xlibris.com
111375

# CONTENTS

# CHAPTER 1

## "Prior to me" years

Hector was my Dad's given name. Unusual in the fact that, that was his only name other than the McGregor last name. He added an E in between to sign his name later on to look more professional he said. In 1915 at the age of 13 years he was given the task of moving the family and livestock from the depressed and oppressed state of North Dakota to the new wide open prairies of Saskatchewan where land was free to homestead to anyone wanting to permanently settle, build a home, and thereby develop the vast country of Canada.

Fortune and a simple way of life awaited all who had the pioneer instinct to do this.

Not so easy though. A tough climate, too cold, too hot, too dry, too wet, winds reaching tornado speed, mud huts, inadequate clothing, horses and mules coaxed into doing too much.

Oh yes, Hector was about to begin a journey that thousands of others can relate to in those land rush days, promoting the movement of people to the prairies of Western Canada.

The destination for Grandpa (Duncan McGregor) was to be Nadeauville, Saskatchewan, a small community settlement 45 miles west and north of Swift Current.

I've always asked why, but the land was free and the opportunity was there, so why not? But it must have been extremely tough to carry out an existence in what I see as a dry, barren, low-yield land of light soil.

However, many settled, many succeeded, and some failed and perished. This was the way of life then.

The bond that was created among the settlers was incredible, a glue that held the community tightly together. This extreme effort by the people of that time created a breed of honest and hard workers, carrying a belief in God and family.

This was exactly what John A. MacDonald dreamed of as a prime minister of Canada. He dreamed of the creation of a country from sea to sea by people who had emigrated from all over the world to live in North America and who could settle in the West and displace the vagabond Indians and keep the aggressive Americans from gobbling up the west from Mexico to Russia.

The railroad was to help the settlers achieve this dream of an Eastern government. It was sort of like, we have a plan now, and you poor people do the work. They did just that. There is no way to describe the effort, sacrifice, and creativity that went into this huge venture of the making of the country of Canada.

Many books by scholars and authors much wiser than me have testified to this period of history. I'm not going to try to rewrite this part of history.

Now back to Hector. When he grew up, he married a Norwegian girl named Clara Carlson. He broke land, farmed with his brothers and sisters, developed land with the McGregor clan to the point where he felt he had done enough for the family, and bought his own farm at Gull Lake, one of the few areas that were not a railroad town. It was located two miles west of the town, which was originally built as an R76 ranch settlement.

Gull Lake was Hector's choice. The land was available, so this was where he became his own master. This was where he had control of his own destiny—a home of his own, a home to raise three boys and three girls, a home where an education was available by way of a school that went to twelfth grade—an education that he never had. He only reached third grade due to the resettling and turmoil of work and survival.

Dreams were plentiful then, and the future held nothing but a promise.

Let me introduce the six children from the oldest to the youngest: Lois, Malcolm, Orville, Vangie, Doreen, and lastly, me, Ron, or Ronnie.

This was where the family became a little *dysfunctional.* The first five were close in years. However, I was fifteen years younger than Lois and six years younger than Doreen. So needless to say, I was kind of an afterthought, a mistake, a gift. I've had all the description of what happened during conception. Whatever, here I am, and this is where the life of Hector McGregor, my dad, gives way to my life, the life of Ron, or Ronnie, or as you will see as this story unfolds, many other names to which I answered and sometimes didn't.

Here we go.

# Chapter 2

## He Doesn't Even Cry

In January 1946, on a cold Wednesday night around 9:00 p.m., the sixth child of Hector and Clara McGregor was pulled into the bright lights of Gull Lake Hospital by the caring hands of a small-town doctor named Dr. John Matheson. This was the last time I would be pulled anywhere without a fight.

The names given to me were *Ronald*, by my grandmother, and *Dwight*, from the Great Dwight Eisenhower, one of the former presidents of the United States.

*A* full-term baby, I weighed seven pounds and nine ounces and was ready to grow. Bundled up safely, I was proudly carried by Mom and Dad (previously Hector and Clara) into our two-story home—two bedrooms on the main, full upstairs for whoever was the hardest to put to bed. It was a small house for eight, but everyone fit for a few years until the oldest started to leave home.

I didn't care as I was being protected at all times by whoever wasn't picking on me at any given moment. If one of my brothers or sisters was being mean, the others would stick up for me. I couldn't lose, so consequently I learned very early how to play one against the other and manipulate to get my own way. In other words, I was spoiled rotten. All my siblings will vehemently attest to this.

Not that I wasn't within my rights sometimes, as when my two sisters, Vangie and Doreen, were obediently pushing me in a baby carriage at the

Victoria Day celebration in Gull Lake. They became sidetracked by friends and forgot about me on the street when a sudden shower filled the carriage with water. Luckily I floated to the surface and survived. They have both long forgotten about this, but I've been told this story by much more trustworthy lips than theirs.

A refusal to dry dishes from my oldest, meanest sister, Lois, resulted in a trip in our Model A Ford to the abandoned open well, where we used to drown unwanted cats as they were born (too many to keep and feed). Into a gunnysack and hung over the top of the well cribbing to be asked, "Are you going to dry the dishes?" "No," I replied repeatedly until she gave up and took me back home. I immediately raced into the house and tearfully told my dad all about it. The shit hit the fan, and I was full of happiness. My revenge was completed with a beautiful beating of my mean sister, Lois.

But that was just the beginning with my big sister, whom I'm sure being fifteen years my senior felt that she was more of a mother than a sister to me. Many times as I was growing up, I was mistaken for a son of my sisters and later on, a son of my sisters-in-law.

An influence which I'm sure had an effect on my future relationships with the opposite sex was the fact that I was the baby—the little one, the brat, the cute little guy with the white blond hair, the one that had a hard time being heard above the crowd of kids older than I was—so I developed in other ways. These sometimes would end up putting me into trouble. I couldn't get out of easily—end up putting me into trouble.

Clara Alida Carlson—my sweet, doting, Norwegian mother—gave me the musical genes, the good-natured side, the emotional, caring side, and the side that probably kept me alive through the messy situations that were to follow in my mixed-up life.

I loved and admired my mother in my early years. She tried so hard to give me the best of everything. I was doted on, never ever disciplined by her, and every need, hurt, ache, or pain was taken care of. We were dirt-poor, and any amount of money that came in was strictly controlled and dished out by my dad, of whom everyone in my family feared. It was a natural fear born of respect but became a fear based on hate as we became older.

My dad's mother, or my grandmother, was also around us until I was going to school. Not that I remember her too much, but I do remember that Dad listened to her. She taught me the basics, such as tying my shoes and buttoning my shirts. Another female influence! As I was growing up, my mom was my companion. Mom and I were home alone most of the time.

Dad and my brothers were working, while my sisters would be either in school or dating or hanging out with their girlfriends.

I got used to being alone. I played alone, created projects alone, took on bigger jobs than I could handle, read, read, and read everything I could get my hands on from school, the library, and whomever I could borrow books.

School was a piece of cake for the first eight years. I didn't know what a final exam was until ninth grade, and I never attended school during the last two weeks of June because I was recommended to the next grade and exempted from writing finals, as was the case every year. Smart? Not really. I think now it was because I read so much to occupy my lonely times that I was prepared for school.

Aside from being the youngest in the family, I was picking up what they were laying down, if you know what I mean. This was also the bad stuff.

Mom bore the brunt of any little failure I'd have. Dad would frown on any accident and screwup. Any little crisis I'd create, the spoiled one, was carried on to her shoulders. Throwing tantrums was the norm when things didn't go my way. Broken toys, broken windows, broken doors, and Mom's broken heart because she never wanted to see me hurt or upset. She was always protecting and consoling me even though I was the cause of my own peril.

I can't remember a time when she gave me shit. Only love and help. Poor Mom. How many times have I tricked her. I'm sure she knew who was wrong but refused to show it to me—a big mistake, but a mistake she made out of love for a child she couldn't figure out.

Mom was thirty-eight and Dad was forty-four when I was born. As I reached my teenage years, that age difference was too much of a gap, especially entering the changes of the '50s and the '60s, as I'll get right into later on.

# CHAPTER 3

## Poor, Poorer, and Poorest

*Poor* was a four-letter word to our family. We hated to admit we were poor. We hated to go to school with clothes outdated, homemade, dirty, and torn and with shoes that people knew were hurting us by the way we walked.

Without much water at our small farm, no running water, no indoor plumbing, no toilets, no power, no telephone, no TV, and just one radio beside Dad's chair in the kitchen with his fingerprints all over it, we were short of many luxuries in life growing up.

Going to school soon made me realize that we were poor, and I hated it. I resented the fact that we were less than others. Fighting to prove I could be better than others soon became my forte. But fighting eventually gave way to outsmarting people. This was where I excelled, and it created in me a feeling of superiority toward people who disdained the lower class such as our family, and it is a characteristic I still put into play today. I loved it then, and I love it now.

I feel that if you can outthink and mentally jab, dance, and prance with the moves of a boxer, you can overcome the class differences people create in a society such as ours. At times, when winning these psychological contests didn't give me the results that I wanted, my feelings turned to hate and revenge, which usually resulted into trouble down the road, trouble I didn't need and couldn't get out of.

Being poor became a catalyst in my life—a catalyst of desire to get ahead, to achieve above and beyond everyone else, to have more and become more, and to want more and never have enough—a characteristic destined to create low self-esteem. Happiness was always at arm's length. Someone always had something better than I had or had more, was better looking, richer, happier, smarter, stronger, and faster. I couldn't win at everything. This would always piss me off, prompting the saying I would always use: "It's better to be pissed off than be pissed on." And believe me, we as the poor McGregor family from two miles west of Gull Lake were many, many times pissed on by the superior, rich people around us.

# CHAPTER 4

---

# My Savior-Booze

Ah yes, that wonderful feeling at the age of eight—that sweet rush of alcohol coursing through my veins and creeping into my brain, making me feel wonderful, smarter, and stronger, and taking me away to the Land of Oz.

I loved it but couldn't get enough at the age of eight. What the hell! I didn't even know how to get what I wanted. Occasions rose, though, when I could steal, connive, and trick people into giving me some liquor, acting funny to make people laugh and give me more. Oh yes, this was my focus for many, many years—this wonderful source of happiness—alcohol. The great equalizer that makes people who are five feet tall become giants within hours. I used to call myself the Stretchy Man—ten feet tall at midnight and two feet tall at dawn.

By the age of fifteen, it consumed me. It became the one nemesis I could not overcome—the devil of my soul. Time after time, I tried to overcome this devil in the bottle, this genie that was so much more cunning than me. It wasn't until my fifty-fourth year in life that I finally won the battle, but I lost so much in the battlefield that I'm not sure yet that I have won the war.

As I relate the stories, you can decide who won.

---

# CHAPTER 5

## Everyone's Shadow

It didn't matter who was around; I was following if that person was allowing it. If it happened to be my sister, there would be two. Girls seem to travel in pairs, sisters or not.

The friends of my sisters also became my friends. This was when I'd become an unwanted pet. Usually though I could tag along for a while before they would rudely tell me to, well, you know the words to that song. I was to learn many of those colorful words and use them well for the rest of my life.

This was how I learned a lot of things growing up with the three sisters and two brothers of mine. Of course, Mom and Dad too, but like I said before, the age difference was such that they weren't quite teaching the things I needed to know in the fast-changing age of the '50s and the '60s that I needed to merge into the fast lane of life.

Should the situation be my sisters, Vangie and Doreen, for instance, there would inevitably be cool stuff such as boys being discussed. The insight I gained here would later prove to be absolutely useless. Their help sucked for me, and as their taste in men changed and developed, so did my life. For that, I would later on be grateful but also resentful and hateful. But we will get to that later on.

During my early years, I was a dress-up doll for my sisters—a live doll they could dress up and laugh at and pretend that I was something their imagination devised with whatever their meager closets held for me to dress up with.

My youngest sister, Doreen, made one of Dad's granaries (empty, of course) into a playhouse. I was one of the puppets she would use to amuse our cousins and her friends for a while until I would get mad at being laughed at and would run away to do more masculine deeds.

God, I hated those theatrical moments! But I'm sure I made them happy for a while in our otherwise boring farm life.

Sleepwalking and talking in my sleep were something I did well, I was told. This scared everyone in our family, including my dad.

We had an upstairs that served as a large bedroom where at least four of us slept, usually the three girls and me. I would always be put to bed first, so I was asleep before everyone else. This was good for everyone else because the brat would be in bed and finally my sisters and brothers could get the attention they so craved from Mom and Dad.

They soon found out that my little mind was resting but not totally stopped. This would sometimes create the ghostlike effects they will remember forever. Outer limit effects. They at first believed that I was awake and doing this on purpose and refusing to believe I was asleep. It was not until the famous night that the show became reality and everyone believed. God, was I glad, but the pain was almost not worth the proving.

There was a two-by-two-foot hole on the floor of the big bedroom, which was also the ceiling of our little living room downstairs. Dad had an oil furnace downstairs in the living room, and the heat duct would go to the bedroom through the floor to keep us warm. However, in the summer, he would just take the duct off the furnace and, forever I will wonder why, he would put a piece of cardboard over the hole in the floor, or ceiling. We always stepped over or around it (except that when you are a sleepwalker, your mind doesn't allow for little things like cardboard over holes on the floor). So you know where I'm going next—straight down, of course. With me ending up with a bloody face and a cracked elbow, everyone woke up screaming, yelling, and crying over me, and literally over me too, as I was lying on the floor in my flowery jimmies that my sisters loved to see me wear. Everyone was blaming everyone, and I was lying there in bewilderment as to what had happened.

Looking back now, I think I know who cared the most about my welfare—my Mom! She held me, consoled me, and quietly calmed everyone else down enough to get them all back to bed quietly. I was okay, and I was the talk of the family for a while. I can't remember if the hole was fixed by anyone, however. We weren't very good carpenters, I guess.

The same upstairs would be a great source of entertainment for all of us and a place where we could all hide in moments of distress. It was a place where my brothers could scheme and plan their attacks on me, I'm sure. I bore the brunt of many of their jokes. It was their war room, their battle planning room, their engineering place where they would devise ways to "get" their little brother. They were like GI Joes, and I was the enemy. Between the age of three and five, I wasn't much of a fighter, but I was all they had to perform their battle exercises on.

Now, they never had creativity, and it's a good thing that they never went to a real war such as bombing. I mean, come on, to hang your butt out the upstairs window and drop the brown stuff on top of me while I was below playing graders and trucks on the little sand box surely didn't take too much intelligent planning, you would think. But they got away with it, and I was naive enough to let it happen more than once. What fun that was! But I loved my little playground out back. I loved to build roads and bridges and to imagine that my one grader, one truck, and my little wagon were many, many pieces when there were only three.

I would emulate my dad. He was operating a grader for the municipality. Our farm couldn't support us so he went to work for a pittance of what he did for them. He was topnotch; this I was told by many later. He was respected by everyone, and he could build a road and maintain it better than anyone before and anyone since then. He had great hands to feather the controls, and the road was perfect behind him. He'd always say, "If you have to do it twice then you shouldn't be doing it." This applies to anything, I guess.

Yes, in those days my dad was my hero. Everything he did, I wanted to do. So I did everything in my playground. It was where I spent endless hours and was happy. I'd put in many hours of unpaid service, but I was happy.

Dad would eventually start taking me with him in his truck to wherever the grader was working. He had a bunkhouse that he pulled, and he would cook, sleep, and eat in it. You wouldn't believe how happy I was to go with him. I would help fuel up the grader, help with the meals, and be his buddy. I was alone with the man I loved and looked up to like a god—my dad. It was something else. He was a totally different person at work. He was a teacher, a confidant, a father, and for me, no one was ever going to say anything bad about my dad because I would get very angry.

That would change, sadly, and his problems would become mine.

# CHAPTER 6

# My First Bus, Love, and Dog

The day I'd been waiting so long for, the day I heard so much about, the day my sisters and brothers rehearsed me for. They briefed me, advised me, drew me pictures and maps, told me horror stories, and probably most importantly, I was their hope that I would be the one that could do better, go further, and succeed where they were failing.

This was school, the first day of the rest of what was to be twelve years of fun and games. At six years and eight months, I was older than most starting that year. Because my birthday was on January 6, I wasn't allowed to start at five years and eight months old by the strict book principal named Ernie Franks. My dad met with him and the school superintendent, but as Dad was poor and a Protestant, there was no letting me start even though I was late for only six days or I could have begun with a whole different bunch of friends.

Did this affect my education? I doubt it. I loved my teacher in first grade. I mean, I *loved* her. She was my Velcro, and I was her cling-on. When I passed into second grade, I wouldn't let go of her, and I cried. God, was I dumb. Even today, I'm embarrassed to think of this part. She had a dark complexion, and she was beautiful, smart, well spoken, and sought after by the male teachers, single and married. But I was her pet, and I felt so special. What a start to an education. It was love at first sight and love in the first grade! It was a one-sided love that kick-started me into learning because whatever she said and told me, I would listen and do. My first teacher was my first love and my favorite memory. Miss Delorme. Oh yes, you will always be on my mind. Thank you, thank you, thank you.

This school in Gull Lake, Saskatchewan, was a two-mile walk from our farm. Many methods were devised to get me there—by horse, car, walk, hitchhike, bicycle—but the new way was the school bus. At first, I loved it. This yellow and black contraption would come to our driveway entrance and pick up my sister Doreen and me. We were the only ones going to school when the bus route started. We had a disadvantage, however, in that we would be the first to be picked up and the last to be let off. Now, come on. How unfair was that? We had two miles to go and traveled forty-two miles morning and night. That was the way. Nothing was about to change for a long time.

This was politics and class. We the McGregors were taken advantage of again. Poor Protestant and stupid, I guess.

I hated those three hours of waste, so Mom would stand by the road and wave at the bus by probably 75 percent of the time until they changed things where I could use two buses: one at the driveway and one coming from Carmichael. Then I only had to ride two miles each way. It didn't take rocket science to figure this little deal out.

Enough about the stupid school bus, the stupid drivers, and the throwing-up, crying students that hated the bus as much as I did for different reasons. Happiness was getting off the bus. Either at school or at home, I was happy with the fact that there was something exciting awaiting.

Let's start with coming home from the bus. I had a dog named Buster. He would be my dog until I was nineteen years old, when he died. He jumped into Dad's truck box one day after work on the grader somewhere up north in Hazlet, Saskatchewan. Dad brought him home unknowingly.

The next day, though, Dad said Buster's going back because he's somebody else's dog. We can't keep him. We were all sad about this, but we understood. We played with him, and he liked us a lot before he left with Dad. Even in that short time, we had named him Buster. My sisters briefly dressed him up in a little dress. He hated it like I hated it. He and I looked at each other at this moment and quite understood.

Dad took him to work again to drop him off where he jumped in, figuring he would 'go where he lived, Dad said. The next day Buster showed up at our place, not by truck though. He walked, ran, whatever. He traveled those forty-something miles back to us. "So," Dad said, "you stupid dog, if you are that dumb of an animal to come here then you'll have to stay here. I'm not taking you back."

This was Dad's way saying, "I'm glad you came back on your own. Welcome, welcome, welcome!"

Buster was as stubborn as Dad, and Dad liked that. He was a cross between a coyote and a German Shepherd, we found out later. He was about a year old, and he was smart big time. He was also very tough. He protected us, especially Mom, as she was home alone a lot.

We lived right beside the old #1 highway, and there were many hitchhikers, vagabonds, salesmen, thieves, and hungry jobless people always coming along. That dog Buster was our security fence, our queen's guard, and our protector. He was always where we needed him. He decided who was coming down that driveway. He was like homeland security to us. He would sort the good from the bad. The bad guys never got through. He was awesome.

He died heroically, and that was one of the saddest days of our lives. He was with us for many years—probably fifteen years—when a pack of dogs led by a Great Dane, owned by the rich Downey family, was killing cattle and roaming the country. Buster wouldn't allow them access to our little farm, so he paid the price. He wouldn't join the game and fought them off. He lived and three of them died, but the chicken Great Dane ran off. Buster was tough.

Buster paid the price in terms of injuries. His eyes were hanging out when he came home, and my good brother, Orville, helped patch him up, and I think Dad cut his eye out. Buster lived for a while, but on my nineteenth birthday, I went into the makeshift bale house we constructed for him, and he was gone to a better place. It was a sad day for us all. I think Dad even cried that day. That day was horrible, but due to the fact that he was suffering and in pain, his death was a blessing to him, but not to me. That cold, windy, sad day was to become a turning point in my life. I mention this now because looking back, I mark my life with these events like starting blocks at the start of a race. Sometimes you get off to a good start, and sometimes you just run with the pack. However, this happened when I was nineteen years old, when Buster, my dog, died, and there were so many things that happened prior to this. That was Buster's story, and I'll never ever forget what he did for our family.

# CHAPTER 7

# Measuring Up

When Dad took me with him to work, I'd get lonely and bored staying in the bunk house by myself. I'd go with him on the grader too, but he'd leave at daylight and be gone until dark. So for me, those days were too long to bounce on his knees or ride on the fuel tank or fall asleep and keep hitting my head on the hard steel frame of the cab. He'd fold his jacket up so I'd have a pillow, but this wasn't good for more than a few minutes. Not comfortable. I wouldn't complain because I was with my dad.

Dad had plans for me, though, and he wouldn't leave me alone unless he felt I was going to be safe. We trusted each other. One of his plans was to talk to a farmer whom he knew had kids my age and leave me there for the day with the family.

Being alone so much at home and with Dad, I didn't know how to act around strangers. So I was very shy and very polite because I wasn't sure of myself. This was about to change, however, when my shyness would become a tool and cocky insolence would be the norm later in life.

Being creative during my lonely playing and being athletic helped me make friends with the new farm kids I met along the roads Dad graded.

The other families all liked Dad because he would do a good job on their roads, and though he wasn't supposed to do it, he would grade their driveways for nothing. He was a good man, they all told me.

Let's meet some of the kids who would later become my schoolmates and sports mates. The McDonalds. The parents were Mr. and Mrs. to me. I'm sure they had first names, but we'll just call them Mr. and Mrs., as I did in utmost politeness.

Bob and Jim were the boys, and they were the ones that were important to me. They were smart, athletic, and lots of fun. I envied them because they were composed of were two boys and one girl named Jeannie. They were close in age, and even then, I could see that they were being brought up right. Their mother dressed them nicely; their dad was strict too, but he was kind and guided them carefully. We'd play for hours, and I learned lots of new ways to pass the time on their farm.

We started school together in Gull Lake. They were to become my competition in everything. We would have sleepovers, and we got along great.

Another family was the Westons. This one was a little different. There was a girl my age, but the boys were younger.

Brenda was the girl, and she was also super smart and bossy. But I really liked her, and she tolerated me being around her farm. I'd do what she wanted me to do, mostly house stuff, but I liked it. Later we would start school in the same year. She was super smart. I would compete with her to achieve the highest average. One year I beat her, and I was extremely happy.

There was no attraction on her part toward me, but she could have asked me to die on my sword and I would have. I had a big-time crush on her. Oh well. I didn't have to die because she never asked me to.

There were some others, but those two families were special to me. Dad knew it and went out of his way to accommodate me sometimes.

This was a good sound base for me as I learned how people lived like that worked hard and were successful. Some of the farmers around Gull Lake were all of that and more. Some did well.

Dad seemed to know who was honestly successful and by way of hard work, and he'd also share his beliefs about who came by success dishonestly. The ones who were crooked (he'd call it) he had no respect for. He would overstate this fact until I formed the same opinion of many people before I was old enough to judge for myself. Judging people from a grader was probably not the best thing for me, but it was to be my early childhood education. This gave me a channel of bitterness that I spent a long time sorting out after. Dad had good things to say about the McDonalds and the Westons. I'm glad he was right.

# CHAPTER 8

# Grade School

You've met Miss Delorme from grade one, the only beautiful teacher I would ever have. No one matched up to her.

Grade one was a breeze. This is where I met thirty-five other kids who were all after the same thing: an education, to learn to be something in life and to learn how to satisfy parents and teachers.

We all got along, and no one failed grade one, although you would deserve to fail. This was good because this system gave you a reason to succeed and have a fear of failing. Nobody was along for a free ride. Even when I was in grade one, I knew I had a gift. I knew I could learn and get good grades.

Everybody was happy. School was a happy place early on. Being good at school was a big deal at home. My high marks made everyone proud of me, and I would try harder.

Grade four was my peak. This was when I beat everyone in with my high average of 96 percent. I won most of the spelling bees, sang in the church quartet and the choir, and sang every Friday at our entertainment hour in front of the class. I played in the school band, traveled to Swift Current, Shaunavon, and Maple Creek for competition. I excelled in track and field, hockey, and baseball. I was rockin'! The world was a pushover, and I was pushing.

School, sports, church, and meeting new people were the main courses of my life in my preteen years. Life was pretty good for me. Actually, these were to be the best years of my life as time would tell.

There were some instances when the previously mentioned demon in the bottle showed up and I found an opportunity to be friends with him when he would come to our lives. He was beginning to come to our house more often, as Dad was drinking more and life was dealing with him with a bad hand. I saw this, and it was pretty hard to sleep sometimes when things would get out of hand.

Orville and Malcolm, my two brothers, would argue with Dad when my sisters were starting to date men, and this created some problems.

Life was changing, and I was too young to realize that life for us McGregors in Gull Lake, Saskatchewan, was soon to be gone as we knew it, life as eight members of a family that ate, laughed, and slept together. That period of our lives was short because of the spread in years between us.

I was somewhat oblivious to the problems developing at home. I wasn't deaf and blind. I was dumb, though, and didn't speak up during any fights. Only when Mom and I were alone would I talk about anything going on. I will say now that Mom was beginning to get worried about losing her girls to men she didn't know and her boys to girls she didn't understand.

The first to go would be Lois, the eldest sister. After a training course in nursing away from Gull Lake, she met and dated the son of a Polish family from south of Gull Lake. They farmed on what was called the Bench Hills.

Coming from a large family, Jim Piechotta was Lois's choice. Lois had black hair, dark eyes, and a great smile, and she was pretty. She was smart and outspoken, and as I said before, bossy and could be mean.

I'm not sure what the attraction was, but Lois and Jim were in love, I guess. I knew nothing about that emotion at that time.

One major problem was about to move front and center in our lives due to this match-up. The Piechotta family was Polish, and we were Scottish/ Norwegian. Oh! Oh!

Catholics versus Protestants. Let the wars begin.

# CHAPTER 9

## Barefoot, Pregnant, and an Oil Boom

Lois was to make the normal transition in life to a higher education in the nursing field. She got a lot of credit for that and was looked up to by the rest of the family. Dad was proud of her, and although he didn't always come across as a loving person, he had pride and love for where Lois was headed. I was too young to understand but was told by him later how proud he was then.

When Jim Piechotta came along, the relationship changed between Dad and Lois. Arguments were more frequent, and Dad's drinking was front and center. Lois hated drinking, and that was that. No fight between them was ever won or lost.

This was funny to me later, as Jim had the same problems with booze as Dad. Perhaps worse, Jim would sometimes become mean and had a lot of pent-up anger that escaped through the cap of the bottle. I'm not going to go as far as saying that the bottle consumed him, but it didn't help his life.

Lois was dating, working, and moving to town to live in Gull Lake and went to work as a telephone operator. I'm not sure what came first, the engagement or the pregnancy, but the wedding was being planned and things were getting tense around the old farm house of the McGregor's.

As I said before, the Polish Piechottas were strict Catholics. We were part-time Protestants. Dad never went to church anyway. Mom tried to get us to church, as she liked the hymns and liked Sundays when she could clean us up and be a little proud of her kids. I liked church too, and my early childhood friend from school, Brenda Weston, also went to our church regularly. I liked that too. She was in the quartet I was part of.

Our religious upbringing was sporadic. We didn't really have much structure. Dad figured all they wanted was money, and the envelope that was sent for donations would eat away at him lying there beside the radio.

I got something out of church, though—singing, praying, and respect from others—because they figured that there may be hope for at least one of the McGregor's.

I look back and wonder where Mom was when I was in church. Most of the time she would just take me, I guess. The two summer church camps I attended were fantastic experiences. Cypress Hills were home of the summer camps, and that was my first stay away from home. Homesick? You betcha, but I got over it and went two years in a row. Trees, water, and religion. Life was good, and summer holidays were shortened by two weeks. Summer holidays I found too long and too boring. School is where I wanted to be, with my friends, with my enemies, and with my teachers! School was the center of my life at that time. That's about it for religion that I can remember.

This is where I got a little confused about the fight that was about to happen when Lois decided to get married. Getting married was okay for Dad, but the "turning Catholic" drove him up the wall. Lois totally committed to the Catholic Church the Piechottas belonged to. I listened to much ranting and raving about this deal. I guess Dad knew that Lois was going to become a devout Catholic and thought she would force religion on everyone. I don't know, but I do know he was furious.

He allowed her the freedom to get married, went to the wedding, and gave her away to Jim Piechotta. Good deal, I thought. Little did I know that later on this turnaround in beliefs would have an effect on my life too.

Things were changing in the '50s. The war was over in 1945. Two world wars and a major depression between 1914 and 1945, with the Korean War thrown in for dessert. This was a hard period of history for everyone at that time. If anyone thinks that this period wasn't tough, then they don't care or they haven't been paying attention to history.

Hector, my dad, was always guilty of the fact that he was too young for the First World War to be conscripted and too old for the Second War. They wouldn't have taken him anyway, as he was the oldest son of a farmer. He still felt guilty and felt he missed out when his buddies went to war and some did not return. The ones that went through it had all these stories to tell over a bottle of whiskey, and the romantic side was intriguing to him. They didn't say too much about the ugly side. They would rather keep that part to themselves. Perhaps they should have told more of that part so that the world wouldn't repeat the mistakes it is making now.

The 1950s were exciting. Then crops were good, and politicians had a vision to finish the building of North America. Money was finally freed up to businesses to build highways, bridges, and houses, to drill for oil, and to employ people in long-term jobs and careers.

The baby boom was on, and everyone seemed to be pregnant from 1946 to the mid '50s. There was love all around. The world deserved this period. "Make love not war" would be the theme. This is what our family did. First, Lois, then Vangie.

Vangie was different in the fact that she quit school and was working for Busse Bros, the hardware store in Gull Lake. Vangie was well liked, smart, and ambitious. She liked to help people and did whatever she could for our family. Whatever money she had left over, she gave to us. There's not much I can think about Vangie to pick on her about.

Until the oil boom at Gull Lake coincided with the building of the Trans Canada Highway. This highway was to go by our house a one-fourth mile south of the old #1 highway.

These two projects would bring an influx of people into the area. Some of these workers would remain to live, some workers would marry local girls, and some would just leave their marks behind.

Rudy Raymond was an oilman. He worked for Anglo American and had been in the war. He was the son of a poor family from Arborfield, Saskatchewan. Originally of French descent, he was gifted with the art of storytelling, mostly true but colored with some gray areas. That's okay. He was funny, and he was very handy with carpentry and electricity, which we needed in a big way. Dad was neither. So Dad liked Rudy for many reasons. Dad didn't use him in the sense that most people would have. Rudy didn't do things for nothing. He was very smart with his money. He had been through tough times, and he swore this wasn't going to happen again.

Vangie and Rudy started dating in 1954. This was when they hung out with a crowd of friends with whom they still are friends. This is how close-knit everyone became in their group.

The closeness in this group of people is notable in the fact that most of them married and had kids from this period.

Vangie and Rudy were two peas in a pod. They became friends, lovers, and married and had a family. This was the way life was supposed to be then. This was the dream of the country, and this dream has proven to be reality for them.

Vangie and Rudy's wedding was a little different from Lois and Jim's. Vangie was quite pregnant at her wedding, so she was dressed in modest clothes, and no false pretenses here. I've always admired and respected her for this. At Justice of the Peace, a small wedding in a banquet room, and lots to eat and drink. Paid for by the groom. Rudy was responsible, and he always met his responsibilities.

Rudy was good for our family, and we welcomed him to the McGregor clan, as we had Jim Piechotta.

Jim and Rudy were two totally opposite characters. Many times I turned to both of these older brothers-in-law for advice and help.

Not always would things be happy and easy, though. There would be times that I would wish that Lois and Angie hadn't married the two clowns. But the good times definitely outweighed the bad times.

I'm not going to single out situations, but events later on transpired to change the course of our family's destiny.

Vangie and Rudy were married in 1955.

Next to walk down the aisle was Doreen. This was shocking to us. Doreen, like Vangie, hung out with Midge Cark, her best friend for life. They met the oil man too. A younger circle than Rudy and Vangie's crowd but the same partying type.

The backseats of the vehicles in the '50s must have been a lot more comfortable then. Doreen came home pregnant, and the wedding was being planned before the dust settled from Vangie's wedding.

Bill Sullivan, a hot-tempered, hardworking well-built short Irishman was Doreen's man of choice. Not to be outdone, Midge Clark was to perform the same miracle of life with Glen Hystad, also an oilman, who was a notch higher when it came to fiery, tough, and fought at the drop of a hat.

I remember one incident when Doreen came home late and Dad had to go to work early. Doreen and Bill sat outside of our house with the car running, music playing, laughing, and probably making love. When Dad had had enough, out the door he went, told Doreen to get her ass in the house, and Bill to leave. Doreen ran in the house embarrassed and crying with Dad kicking her butt all the way across the kitchen, living room, and upstairs to our bedroom where I was sleeping. I thought it was funny, but Doreen didn't and cried all night.

Doreen got married in the fall of 1956, one year after Vangie. She too carried an extra few pounds down the aisle of matrimony. Doreen was married in white. This was what she dreamed of as a little girl. She was happy. She worked, worked, and worked to make a good life and proved everyone wrong.

The cards were not in her favor, and as time would go forward, she found out how tough marriage and life could be.

Five years were to go by before another wedding took place. I guess too much time had gone by, so God decided there would be two for one in '61.

Both Orville and Malcolm married within one week of each other. Orville was wed in Webb, Saskatchewan, while Malcolm was married in Drayton Valley, Alberta.

The first wedding was Orville's. His bride was Sheila Parker. Let's introduce Sheila. She was the second of two daughters born to June and Russ Parker. June was a schoolteacher in Webb. June was all class. She knew clothes, furniture, style, and hair. She knew how to match things and make them look right. She was intelligent, whereas others were just smart. She transposed this to her two daughters, Shirley and Sheila.

Shirley was to become more like June than Sheila. Sheila was to pick up what she needed, but she had a quick temper and a fantastic sense of humor. She would use that temper to put you on guard. What Sheila had more than anyone I'd ever known or have ever known was an obsessive-compulsive attitude toward cleanliness. Unbelievably, she also expected this of others. Most of the time she would be helpful and show people how to dress, clean, and even set a table. This sometimes would rub people the wrong way. But I can't remember anyone telling her to her face to get lost. She had that effect on people. They weren't sure how she'd react, so they kept quiet, probably because they knew she was right. She loved to argue and usually won.

These qualities I'm sure attracted Orville to her. She was totally different from anyone in his life. He was in love, and there was no turning back.

Russ Parker was Sheila's dad, a funny, hardworking man who worked with our dad for the municipality of Webb. They built many roads together. The new elevator grader was to be the new road-building machine. This grader had an elevator that would disc the clay from the ditch, and on a moving belt take the clay, rocks, and dirt up to the crown of the road. They would then just grade it flat, and there was your road. Russ Parker and Hector McGregor had this down pat. They worked, drank, and lived together, building roads and earning very little money for what they did.

Orville started working for the RM of Webb too. He too began running a grader. Both Dad and Orville ran graders for twenty-five years each. Dad worked for the RM of Gull Lake and RM of Webb. Orville worked for the RM of Webb and RM of Swift Current.

Both were to be terminated in the same way—very messy and in the most gutless of methods.

RM stood for Rural Municipality of Gull Lake, Swift Current, Webb, et cetera. Each area had its own Councilor or Reeve. These municipalities had served the provinces very well. Money was distributed by the province to be used to build infrastructures in the community. These Councilors are elected by the landowners or farmers to represent them.

This was where it got political sometimes. At times, the difficulty was getting people to step up and do their part. The pay for this was small, but the prestige and inside influence helped some farmers get a leg up on land use, roads to their own advantage, and power. For some, this was to be the way they could exercise power over others.

To test his character, give a man power. Some little men became giants within these structures.

Hector, Orville, and Russ Parker faced some of these power struggles daily. Some councilors with no experience gave orders in road construction. This made things difficult because they did have control.

In the early years of building roads, this system was good. Everyone was building their farms, fences, and dugouts, and they were used to trails and rough going.

Twenty years later, farms and roads were established to the point when traffic was heavier and faster. The equipment they were working with wasn't being updated, and yet Hector and Orville were expected to keep up to the ever-increasing maintenance with very little increase in salary.

The councilors would make their operators reapply for their jobs each spring. This kept the wages in check. It also caused bitterness among equipment operators. The end of grader operating for Hector came in 1967 and for Orville in 1977, one quarter of a century for each.

No pension, no letter of thanks, no severance pay, and no gold watch. Just a note slid under the door at night saying that their services were no longer needed. Oh well, what to do. Move on to better things. Orville did that, but Dad (Hector) was sixty-five, and he was finished. This was the end of a strong man. I'll show this sad ending later in the story.

Sheila, Orville's bride, entered into the municipality world because her dad was running the grader, but now her husband would be doing the same thing. Did she become attracted to grader men? I think not. Orville was a good-looking man. He had red hair, and he was strong, caring, and helpful. He liked to party, but he was responsible and held his job in high regard.

Orville was the only one in the McGregor family with red hair. We used to joke that he got mixed up in the hospital and Dad brought home the wrong baby.

Orville's then Malcolm's were a turning point, for this meant I was the last one to be with Mom and Dad.

Malcolm started working when he had had enough of school by delivering fuel for BA in Gull Lake. He liked his truck delivery and wore his chauffeur's badge proudly on his belt. Dad figured this was a good job too.

For a period of time everyone was working and living at home. I was in school, and everything was going pretty well. Hector still had a handle on things.

# CHAPTER 10

## Drayton Valley—Another Oil Boom

Hector was confused as to how the oil could draw men from one part of the country to another. "Big money," he always called it. This wasn't all there was to it, however. There was excitement, opportunity, and risk. Risk was the key, the chance of doing something new and developing a way of life by putting everything on the line.

Rudy and Vangie were the first to move from Gull Lake to Drayton Valley. The oil boom in Gull Lake was petering out, and Drayton Valley's was beginning. Many moved on to Drayton Valley for promises of a bigger pay. This eventually turned out to be positive, but there were hard times ahead. Many difficulties arose that no one could have dreamed of.

The next to follow were Bill and Doreen. Why? I'm not sure, because Bill went from one service station job in Gull Lake to the same job in Drayton Valley.

The next to go was Malcolm. The same situation developed when Malcolm went from delivering fuel and pumping gas in Gull Lake to doing the same thing in Drayton Valley.

This brought out the worst in Hector, my dad. I watched sadly as Malcolm told Dad he was quitting his job in Gull Lake and going to Alberta. This was a hard thing to watch. Malcolm was downgraded that day. He stood his ground and left crying but determined. Little did I know then, but this similar scenario was about to develop in my life later.

This put Rudy, Vangie, Bill, Doreen, and Malcolm all in Drayton Valley. Malcolm was about to meet Rosalie Robinson of Drayton Valley, the daughter of a landowner and businessman running Cats, which cleared land and leases.

Rosalie and his brother, Billie, were living at home. Rosalie was working as a secretary for the huge Pan American Oil, which had control of the oil play in Drayton Valley or what they called the Pembina Play.

Rosalie was everything Malcolm wanted in a woman—quiet, pleasant, levelheaded, and someone he could lean on for the rest of his life.

The marriage of these two would finally bring Hector and Clara (Mom and Dad) to Drayton Valley to see that their three children—Vangie, Doreen, and Malcolm—perhaps had done all right by moving from Gull Lake. He was right, and life was good for a while.

The boom turned to gloom when the drilling stopped and money was in short supply.

As in any oil boomtown, the activity is phenomenal in the beginning. One new discovery well signals a big play. Oil companies are connected through the stock market, and the game is played by advertising a new discovery to raise more capital to drill. All oil companies are aware of what is happening and send out scouts to see firsthand what is really going on where all the excitement is. In this case, the excitement was in Drayton.

The scouts were a different breed, and they definitely earned their money. All kinds of tricks were employed to get information for the engineers and the executives of the oil companies in Calgary and Houston, Texas. Eventually the money men in New York and Toronto would decide if the incoming information was good enough, then the action would really take place in whatever town happened to be close to the discovery well.

Scouts were the most hated men in the oil patch. They were necessary, but they were spies, and everyone felt that they were selling their souls to the big and rich. Many bar fights and chases through the bush were witnessed where these scouts were discovered.

Mud was the enemy of Drayton Valley. The years 1954, 1955, and 1956 were wet ones with heavy rain and big snow melting into late spring. Drayton Valley was mostly house trailers, skid shacks, and houses built on foundations with no basements. Any roof would do to house the workers that support the oil patch.

Such was the life of Rudy and Vangie, Bill and Doreen, Malcolm and Rosalie, and of course, their friends who had moved from Gull Lake, Saskatchewan, where the boom was smaller but the smell of money was the same.

Rudy and Vangie were a little more fortunate in the fact that Rudy had a small nest egg to buy a new house trailer of a decent size to actually be able to turn around in and not brush the walls doing it. Being an electrician and handy with a hammer and saw, Rudy began with the best that was available then.

The picture faded with Bill and Doreen. All that they could afford to rent was a skid shack five miles west of Drayton.

Malcolm rented a room until he got married and rented a small house on his father-in-law's land.

This was the setting for Vangie, Doreen, and Malcolm, the two daughters and son of Hector McGregor. Everyone back home thought this was wonderful. Why not when the stories we heard from letters written by them and scattered visits back to Gull Lake attested to the fact that life was good. Jobs were plentiful, trailers were the way to go, families were starting, and the future was bright.

This was what we heard from them. Probably this was mostly true. Anything they had at that time was a step up from our small house with a partial dirt cellar, banked with dirt and tarpaper every fall to keep the wind from blowing through the walls. Yes, I am sure things were better in Drayton Valley.

Vangie and Rudy were the first to move to Drayton Valley. Rudy's brother, Sam, was the proud owner of a plane. He loved to fly and one day he had a crash just east of Gull Lake and was killed. This was a great tragedy to Rudy. He was very close to Sam and the move from Gull Lake was probably therapeutic for Rudy.

There were back-and-forth trips for Rudy and Vangie. Their firstborn was Terry the Terrible as I called him. He was probably the most active, trouble-bound, and strongest child I ever saw and would ever see in the future. You could never think of the things that he could get into. One year after he was born, Vangie and Rudy came to Gull Lake from Drayton Valley.

Vangie had a pain in her side and stomach. Dr. John Matheson, who had so kindly pulled me into the world of the McGregor's, examined Vangie and declared she had a cyst that would have to be looked after back in Alberta. He said that the trip back would be fine. In route to Drayton Valley, Vangie became very, very sick. Edmonton was closer than Drayton Valley so into Edmonton they went, where it was discovered the cyst was not a cyst but a burst appendix. Vangie was knocking on death's door, and Rudy was in a panic. Sam's death was bad enough, but to lose his new bride would be a disaster for him.

Whether he got Dad (Hector) the message by telegraph, by phone, or through a neighbor or friend I'm not sure, but we got the information somehow, and the solution to the problem was me. "Could Ronnie come to Edmonton to babysit Terry the Terrible while Vangie is in the hospital?"

"Well sure," Dad said.

They decided to send me on a train from Gull Lake to Edmonton. Great! I was excited at ten years old. I was barely out of babyhood myself. At any rate, I was taken to the train station and put on the train by myself. Luckily, a girl neighbor by the name of Ella Wilson was also going to Alberta on the same train.

She was into boys at that stage of her life, but I felt more at ease that there was someone I knew on that train. The conductor was nice too, and I'm sure Dad had a chat with him about what was going on.

This was my first trip away from home alone. I was not exactly a world traveler, but my eyes were wide open. A virgin of the rails. A virgin of anything at ten years old.

Rudy met me at the railway station in Edmonton, and off we went to the cheap hotel where the infamous Terry the Terrible was being held hostage.

I was not allowed in the hospital, so I didn't get to see my sister Vangie, who helped us so much in Gull Lake. I didn't have time to worry about her too much, however.

My job was simply to stay with Terry, the one-year-old whom I would just have to keep an eye on and entertain while Rudy was in the hospital with Vangie.

Now, there were no telephones, no cell phones, no television, and no radio, just a room with a bed, sink, toilet, and a locked door. Rudy was kind enough to leave books, but Terry was not about to be read to. He ran and ran and ran. The room, a nine-by-six with a bed in the center, didn't take too long to run around for a boy who I'm sure now had ADD.

This constant running, screaming, and never-ever sleeping to give me a break would now come to an end when his face hit the pipes under the sink and the wall turned red from the blood spraying out of his nose and mouth.

I panicked and had no clue what to do. Luckily, I thought of the desk clerk and ran to get help. He came immediately and helped me through the crisis. Terry the Terrible was saved, and this also slowed him down enough that I could control him with the fear that the same thing could happen if he didn't quit running around.

Terry's life was to take on many, many disasters, which I'm sure would make a book with much worse stories as struggled through life.

This was the beginning of travel for me. From Edmonton, Rudy drove me back to Gull Lake and didn't go to Drayton Valley at that time. This was going to happen later.

Rudy and Vangie were very grateful that I was able to help out at that time. I was grateful to God and the doctors in Edmonton that my sister Vangie survived what could have easily killed her, the cyst that became a poisonous venom from a burst appendix.

# CHAPTER 11

## A Friend, a Cop, a Mentor, and a Tormentor

Life for me on the farm two miles west of Gull Lake seemed isolated when I was small. Two miles seemed a long way. Transportation was walking, horse riding, hitchhiking, and bicycling. This was prior to the age of sixteen and prior to driving on my own.

As I became older during the ages of thirteen, fourteen, and fifteen, I was very creative when it came to getting back and forth from "town," as what we called Gull Lake.

I was heavy into sports, so I was either picked up by coaches and brought home or I would stay in town to play whatever sport the season dictated. After the game, I would hang out at the pool hall and beg for a ride home, sometimes doing homework in the pool hall.

The pool hall was owned by a happy-go-lucky robust big man by the name of Kelly Holtby, who had a set of twins by the names of Dale and Gayle. They were a very likeable family, and they probably felt sorry for me hanging out at the pool hall. I was allowed to be in there but not allowed to play pool.

I'd get around this rule by coming in the backdoor, where there was a smaller table with a dim light on top. I would play undetected for a while until I was quietly racked up by Kelly and pleasantly told to quit. I had great respect for the Holtbys, and Kelly would grudgingly drive me home if someone didn't come by before he locked up. His son Dale would be long gone to their home by this time to do his homework, where I should have been. Kelly's daughter Gayle was never around the pool hall.

The pool hall was across the main street of Gull Lake from the Clarendon Hotel. These were two of the most active nightspots in Gull Lake. The other was Speed Café. These three places were active for all ages. They had three separate identities. The hotel had drinking and fighting. The pool hall had games-pinball, pool, and gambling. The restaurant had food, music by way of jukebox, girls by way of waitresses, and hangouts.

Other businesses did well in Gull Lake, but these three were the excitement and character of the '50s and '60s.

At fourteen, I was the owner of a balloon-tired used bicycle, which was already worn out and not too reliable for the trips back and forth town. Tired of the breakdowns, I spied a new bicycle at Busse's hardware store, where my sister had worked. I talked to the clerk and asked him if I could buy it on time. This started a line of credit to purchase something I couldn't afford to pay for with cash that would repeat thousands of times into the future.

My source of income at this young age was my family allowance. Each month I would sign over my check for this sleek bicycle.

Every good weather day I rode on this new bicycle the two miles between the farm and town.

The red and white bike served me well, but there were more bad weather days than good. This was the way of travel for me. This was where I headed on a late cool fall afternoon after hockey practice. This day however I decided to walk a different street and headed north off the normal path for me.

Walking a few blocks north, I came upon a boy playing by himself what we all played at that time-street hockey. I didn't have to wonder why he was playing by himself because I knew who he was, Jack O'Connor, the son of the town cop, Dick O'Connor.

His reputation had him pegged as someone I didn't want to know. The only times I had ever paid any attention to him was when there were about twenty other kids chasing him home trying to catch him and probably beat him up. He was trouble. He was also a year exactly younger than I was. My birthday was January 6, 1946. His was January 6, 1947. We traveled in different circles up to this day I chose a different path.

The other time I paid attention to him before this day was when Dub Henderson, our elementary school principal, threw Jack into the boxing ring. The aggressive principal had built it in the basement of our school to teach boxing and settle fights with gloves on, so there was less chance of injury and there was an audience to witness a winner, a loser, or a coward.

Jack was thrown in and told by Dub to fight someone his own size. I think Jack was intimidated by the people around the ring. I was surprised, but at any rate, Jack wouldn't fight at that time. It would be many years later that Jack and I fought each other, but not at fourteen and thirteen years of age.

The day that I met Jack on the street was a memorable one. I think now that we both needed a friend, friends we became, and as you will see, our lives became interconnected in many ways.

After playing a little one-on-one hockey in front of the O'Conner's house, I was invited in by Jack to warm up and meet his mom and dad. His sister, Pat, wasn't at home at that time. I would meet her, but not that she chose to.

I knew from the moment I walked into the O'Conner's home that this was what I needed: a home away from home, with electricity, telephone, running hot and cold water, a shower and bathtub, and most importantly, a television. They had it all. I knew people had the same luxuries, but this was the first time I had access to the amenities of life. This was like being jettisoned into the future.

The biggest impact on me was made by Jack's mother, Kay. She was special in the fact that she was terrific in all that she did. She was a great mother, a friend to all she met, a hard worker holding a job as a grocery clerk eight to ten hours per day, doing housework, making meals, and doing all the housekeeping chores needed to be done every day.

Jack and Pat were lucky in the sense that their mother, Kay, doted on them and had so much to give them as they were being raised as children of Dick O'Conner, the only town cop in Gull Lake. This in itself was a big chore for her. The constant phone ringing, the problems arising from police work, the stigma of being the town cop's wife—she took it all in stride. She had the instincts and personality to handle whatever came around.

She welcomed me with a friendliness I was not accustomed to. I could talk and talk and talk to her for hours, and she never let on that I was boring or not wanted.

Many nights after that first day of meeting Kay, I was told to sleep over rather than go to my own home. There were always clean sheets and a warm bed. I was blessed to have two moms who cared.

Dick, Jack's dad, being the town cop, was much different. He was strict but fair. He was tough but softhearted. He was smart in figuring a person out, as a cop should be, but education failed him, as he spent a five-year stretch in World War II overseas as part of a tank artillery unit in Europe. Dick was perfect for the role of town cop of Gull Lake.

Known as a street fighter, Dick was never beaten in a one-on-one battle in a fistfight. The town needed a policeman and approached Dick. He was reluctant to do this job, but like every other poor farmer, he needed a job too. He learned as he went and commanded the respect of everyone in Gull Lake and proudly wore the uniform supplied to him. He wore his badge with honor and always sported a holstered .38 caliber revolver and billy club.

These were the police constables of the day. They worked hand in hand with the RCMP. Dick had use of the town jail of one cell to house the drunks, the peace-disturbing types, and transients with no money but needed a place to sleep for the night. Dick had a time and place to do his part for the community, and he served well until he retired with his honor intact.

The one remaining family member to meet was Pat, Jack's sister. Pat, being Jack's older sister, had the upper hand. From my point of view, Pat was favored by Dick, and Jack was cherished and spoiled by Kay. Not that either parent shamed or mistreated either child, but as in many families, kids got away with more from one parent than the other.

Pat was a free spirit. She did what she liked to do. She didn't do things to put her dad on the spot but took things to the limit. If manipulating a boy to get an upper hand on a female competitor, this was fair. Being small in stature, she more than made up for the small part by being witty and quick with the tongue. Such is how we met. She came storming into their house through the porch and loudly asked, "Where the hell did all those boots come from? I can't even walk into my own house anymore."

There was only one more pair of boots in the porch, but this was her way of saying there was one too many pair. I learned early how to deal with Pat. Let her speak first and don't interrupt. Speak only when asked to speak, and never raise your voice to her. These were my rules. They worked, and I was tolerated by her. When I would come to their house and she would answer the knock on the door, she would say, "Oh, it's just you. I thought it was somebody important."

If the door was left ajar, I knew I could come in, and I don't remember being shut out.

In our later years, Pat and I would still fight for fun, but we will always back each other up when necessary. It was a long road to submission, but she became one of my favorite characters eventually.

# Chapter 12

## The Infamous Sixties That Changed All Who Survived the Turbulence of Change

January 6, 1960, brought on two birthdays: one for Jack, my new bud who will be brought to the teen years at thirteen, and me, who was one year older, so fourteen was to be my starting point to the sixties. We were both locked into the starting blocks and ready for the gun to fire and propel us into the next era.

Let's put aside all the athletics Jack and me were into then: baseball, hockey, football, and track and field. We were totally into all these activities, but another pastime appeared at this time—a cheap acoustic guitar, a silver-toned six-string acoustic that sounded terrible to anyone who was listening. To Jack and me, any sound that came from that guitar was wonderful; of course, any sound that was in tune and made music. We both loved this sound from the cheap guitar. However, we had to improve, and this of course took practice, practice, and more practice.

Upstairs in Jack's house was our practice room. This was our music studio, our dream room to dream and emulate every rock-and-roll star of the generation: Buddy Holly, the Ventures, the Fireballs, the Rolling Stones, the Animals, and of course, the Beatles. They were our heroes and proved to be everlasting heroes as the years went by. They excited us, gave us energy, and gave us a new outlet to pass our time and try to create something new.

One guitar wasn't enough, however, so I somehow dug up enough money to purchase another cheap guitar to learn to play along with Jack. We would learn a song, and I would go home to my farm and practice for many hours to get better. My mom loved this because she also played the violin or fiddle and the harmonica. She appreciated music and came from an old-time band of the Carlson family that played for dances all around the Tompkins, Nadeauville districts.

I was lucky in this respect because Dad wasn't into music. He listened to the news on the radio and sports but had no musical inclination. However, he liked to see Mom and me making music. We would play "Love Me Tender," "The Old Rugged Cross," and any of the easy stuff. We weren't perfect, but we sounded pretty good. This was the happiest I ever saw my mom, and this is a memory I cherish.

Jack's mom was also happy that we were upstairs, where she could keep an eye on us, and we weren't uptown getting into trouble. How she put up with the noise and the repeated mistakes that we made to get a song right is pretty unbelievable. But she sat downstairs listening and hoping the music would soon stop and I would go home finally.

When we got enough songs down pat and decided we would play for people, we needed a break song for intermission. The song we chose was "Let's Go." It was a catchy, quick tune that would signal a break was coming up. We used this song for years in our band. This song made Jack's mom, Kay, happy too. She'd say to herself, *Oh good, they're leaving.* "Let's Go" would be played over and over and over. Finally, she realized we were only practicing and not really going. She told this story many times to her friends.

The guitars we learned by practicing, going to watch other guys play, and asking if they could teach us some licks. These guys were the Girodats. Bud, Alec, and Ron traveled as a trio, and they could all play and sing. Drinking was also their nemesis. They didn't have steady jobs and bummed money to support their habits. However we learned some good things on the guitar, especially from Bud. He was talented and could sing very well. I envied him, and looking back, I envied another trait of the Girodats. The drinking, I picked up that trait as well.

Another teacher was my brother-in-law's brother, Irwin Piechotta, who was more professional than anyone around Gull Lake. He was cool. He would play on the radio in Moose Jaw live with only his guitar and sing.

I would phone him and ask if I could come to visit and learn some guitar songs. He would always oblige if he wasn't busy. Somehow, I would get to his house on the farm south of Gull Lake on what we called the Bench. He would try to teach me, but he was so far ahead that I would just sit in awe of him and wonder how I would ever be that good. I never did get that good on the guitar, not even today. He was gifted, and he tragically ended his own life at a young age to the shock and dismay of everyone who knew this prince of a man named Irvin.

There were others such a George Bartole, who was a radio/TV repairman trained musically in the classical guitar. But Jack and I couldn't read music; we played only by ear. This frustrated our music teachers in school because we did very poorly in music class. They weren't teaching us rock and roll. We weren't interested in Mozart and Bach and the language of music.

The world was full of music then: Johnny Cash, Roy Orbison, Elvis Presley, Marty Robins, and Hank Snow! The radio was full of beautiful sounds, new sounds, and exciting beats, and it seemed like there was someone new discovered every day of the sixties.

This was the table that was set for Jack and me. However, we needed two more people to sit at this table with us: another guitar player and a drummer. Without a bass guitar and a drummer, we wouldn't be able to form a rock-and-roll band. However, Gull Lake wasn't that flush with these particular people we needed.

We decided that in order to get these two people, we would have to make them learn as we did with the guitars.

First was the drummer. However, we didn't have drums to try out anyone. We bought drumsticks and used a garbage can. We tried out several guys to see if they had a natural beat. There were lots of banging and noise but no beat. Finally, we decided Terry Smart would be our drummer, the son of the owner of the restaurant on the highway. He did not have a clue, but he was cute. He loved music and had a good-looking sister. He was the chosen one. We worked and worked with Terry. We got a cheap set of drums and finally we could see he was going to be all right. This was exciting because we were making music.

Somewhere in the period of teaching Terry, we were lucky that the United Church brought in a new minister by the name of Cunningham. Originally from England the son of a minister named Ed came to Gull Lake with a guitar in hand. He knew how to play and was into the Stones, the Beatles, and the Animals, of course. Coming from Liverpool and all that good stuff, he was the one we were waiting for.

He joined in with us as a singer and rhythm guitarist. Jack played lead, and I also played rhythm guitar. Terry was a drummer only, but he was getting good and could play "Wipe Out" as a solo, so we were on our way.

We still needed a bass guitar, so in order to do that, I bought a four-string bass and amplifier from Sears and decided I would learn bass.

Between the four of us, I learned to play the bass runs well enough to make our sound good enough to start playing for dances, functions, and of course, money. We were now professionals—we got posters made, booked halls to play in, and away we went like a foursome of gypsies playing for money in front of people waiting and paying us to play.

The players were now in place. The four pieces to a band of dreams. Dreams we all had to be like our rock-and-roll heroes. We started with nothing but dreams and blind ambition. We picked everything up by ear. We used no music sheet because we didn't have time to learn how to read music. This would limit us eventually, but we all felt the beat, and the sound flowed through to make music. And music we did with passion.

As we practiced and got better, we invited friends to listen. They loved it and encouraged us. We bought better equipment and learned more songs to play in front of people.

A talent show was happening at the Gull Lake Elks Hall one night. We all bought Beatles wigs and performed. We won third prize, and we were amazed at the response of the crowd. The older people still didn't appreciate the sound of rock and roll and especially the Beatles. "Long-haired little bastards," some called them. We didn't care what the older generation thought about rock and roll. We knew this music was the real deal. We could feel it. In fact, the more the older complained the better we felt about our generation and our music. We rebelled, and the world was ours in the sixties. Songs like "Live for Today," "Eve of Destruction," "Get off of My Cloud," and "Nowhere Man" were songs we all knew and believed in. How could the world stop us? They couldn't, wouldn't, and didn't stop the revolution prompted by rock and roll.

When we stood in front of the crowd that first time to play, we felt nervous, but we felt another feeling: power. We felt good, and this gave us confidence to go on to achieve more.

This little talent show gave us a desire to be a better band, and we practiced to that end. We thought of a name: the Vibratos. This is the lever on a guitar that pushes the strings to make a sound vibrate and make a wavering sound and is used by all great guitar players. The Vibratos were the start of our career. Short in duration of four years but long in the life of memories of good times.

As we progressed as a rock band, we had responsibilities. Posters had to be made, halls had to be booked, and arrangements had to be made to set up dates and play in places. Advertising, admission fees, travel arrangements, dress clothes, or uniforms had to be made or bought. In those years, most bands dressed alike and looked the same. Individuality wasn't popular yet.

All of these things created much discussion and some fighting, but we put it all together to start off. We played our first dance at the Webb Community Hall. We got our equipment into the hall early and set up. We brought a ticket taker by the name of Bob Davies. He was personable and big enough to be a ticket taker, collect the money, and be a persuasive bouncer by using his way with words and not hurting anyone.

Bob Davies was not musically inclined, but he would become intertwined with Jack and me forever. He was a big part of our future.

As we played that dance, we could feel the tension in the crowd. The music was playing great, and the crowd was into what we were playing. They wanted more. We only had a short list of songs, but we played them over and over, and no one seemed to mind.

As we were playing, a guy by the name of Gerry Castle was pissing in the cloak room where everyone hung their coats. My brother-in-law, Jim Piechotta, was also standing there. Castle was drunk, of course, and Jim said, "What the hell are you doing?" Castle was a shit disturber of the best caliber, and the fight started. And fight they did. There were three groups of people. There were kids from Swift Current, Webb, and Gull Lake.

All three groups hated each other. This was a war from past experiences, but this was the perfect place, and the fight spread throughout the dance hall. There were no police in the little community of Webb, which was twelve miles east of Gull Lake and between Gull Lake and Swift Current.

The police would always cruise dances, but they didn't know about this one or didn't care about it.

However, the first fight was on until we didn't know how to stop it. Blood was flying chairs were coming out, and knives and boots were threatening to kill someone. All we could do was send Bob Davies to call the cops. He ran to a house to phone, but they were partying, so he took his shoes off to go in. But when Ez Lloyd, whose place he was phoning from, found out he was calling the RCMP, Ez literally kicked Bob out of the house, and Bob ran back to the dance hall in bare feet.

The next stop was to shut off the breaker to pull all the power and shut the lights off. We did this and it helped, but we forgot to pick up our guitars and amplifiers. So we had to turn the power back on to do this, and the fight continued. We were scared so we gathered up our stuff, turned the power off, and left. The cops as far as we know never showed up. No one died, but there were a few injuries, and some ended up in the hospital.

This began our career and a lesson learned. We always let the cops know when we were in town. In fact, we would hang a poster up in the police station of each town right beside the wanted posters to let them know most of the time. The cops were our enemies, but it was comforting to know that they were there when we needed them.

As we learned more music, we became more confident in playing more complex music and watched closely the way other bands performed. One of these bands was the Cavaliers from Medicine Hat led by a super guitarist named

Klaas Kraats. They performed all around Alberta and Southern Saskatchewan. They were a class act, were a little older, and had all the up-to-date Fender equipment that was necessary to make the best sound. We envied them.

Klaas Kraats boomed his voice over the PA system powered by three hundred watts and said, "So we understand the Gull Lake has its own rock band starting up called the Vibratos. How would you boys like to come up and play a set while we take a break?" Well, I'll tell you what, we could have crawled out the door but the crowd wouldn't let us. So up the stage we went, picked up those beautiful guitars, and Terry sat behind the full set of drums.

Everything was in perfect tune, and when everything is perfect, the sound is like heaven. We played three songs—"Apache," "Tequila," and "Sloop"—of the John B. The crowd went crazy. That helped us out later because people could see we could perform with the best, and the Klaas Kraats band called the Cavaliers from Medicine Hat were the best at that time. Klaas became famous on his own later in Calgary, and we were to meet him again several times. We were happy, excited, and full of ideas. Life revolved around music. Ed Cunningham was the most creative, and Jack had the talent to play anything Ed came up with. Terry and I just learned and accompanied them to fill in the sound. I wasn't too bad on rhythm guitar. I had a fast hand to play a double rhythm, but the bass was something I had to practice a lot to get good at. I made a lot of mistakes, but I was adequate. We played ad lib, told jokes, played songs like "Long Tall Texan" with cowboy hats. We brought kids up to the stage, let them do funny things, and tried to make the crowd part of the music.

Those kids of the day loved it. We were invited to play for dances in other towns for school functions, and we were busy.

We decided that the Vibratos was a name that would never catch on, so we decided to change it to Jack and the Rippers. This gave us a different meaning. From clean cut, dressed the same in stretch pants, and the nice boy image, we became tougher, rougher, and a little dirtier. The Stones, the Animals, and the Rebels were now our types. This was when Terry smartly decided he was going to quit school and go to work on seismographs.

We needed a new drummer. This time we knew how to train someone. This one was easy. He was Gerry Voll, Jack's cousin from Shaunavon, Saskatchewan.

This town was thirty miles south of Gull Lake on the #37 highway. Shaunavon was bigger than Gull Lake, and all sports teams were our competition. We had a good, healthy, competitive relationship through football and hockey and surprisingly, not too many enemies in Shaunavon.

Gerry Voll's father owned the motel in Shaunavon named Voll's Motel. We would play and practice until Gerry got very good on drums. He had drums and knew more about the sound of drums than we did.

So we had a new name—Jack and the Rippers—a new drummer, and a new look. Jack was a good artist, and he would draw cartoon characters on t-shirts with the sleeves cut off. We would wear these over the shirts and jeans we're in, so we had a tougher image.

Jack was well muscled and heavier than the rest of us. He was our lead guitarist and leader of the band. Jack was an excellent fighter, and we were always confident in troublesome situations that Jack could handle it.

This gave me a reason to create trouble later on because I knew Jack would back me up. Many times later on Jack was to bail my ass out of trouble.

Gerry Voll was our new drummer, but he was also our inside tracker to a new crowd. The Shaunavon people were great to us, and we were invited to play for dances through Gerry's connections. We could never have made it without him.

This was when girls came into the picture. The girls of Shaunavon . . . *oh my*! This was a smorgasbord of the best kind. There were girls all over that town, and we met most of them.

We weren't the only ones from Gull Lake to find this out. There were many other guys our age traveling that #37 highway to Shaunavon for the good times and the girls. We used to cruise the town with the foxtails, whip aerials, the fender skirts, the sun visors, and loud mufflers, and the girls would be walking on the sidewalk waiting for us to talk to them into getting in to our cars and going for a ride. Bootleggers, girls, and cars were the order of the day. Times were good and the world was ours.

Girls, guitars, booze, cars, football, and love in the backseat . . . beautiful. God gave us the sixties, and believe me, we made the most out of them.

Some of the girls that we met were special. One of them was Marilyn Nadler. She was the daughter of Bill Nadler who owned Nadlers Men's Wear. They were of strict Jewish religion, upstanding in the community, and strict with their daughter, Marilyn.

Jack met Marilyn at a girls' place named Ann Park one night when we were stormed in and couldn't get back to Gull Lake. There was no romance, but they got to know each other. Later they would date and become very close—too close, I thought. That was the first time I was jealous, not because I liked Marilyn, but because Jack had someone else now and I felt left out.

I saw all of her attributes. She was pretty, smart, and had class. She was what every boy would want in a girlfriend. But inside I was burning up. I was always nice to her but never close to her.

Helping the situation were other girls. One girl was Brenda Olson of Olson's Hardware, also in Shaunavon. She was my friend. She was like Marilyn and was respected and well brought up. I liked her a lot, and Jack and I spent a lot of time with these two girls.

There were others as well. Like I said, the town was like a smorg. There was Julie Houston, the butcher's daughter; Ann Park, Lynn Hooper, Sandra Ogden, Sandra Behrman, and Gina Gryde, the main ones that we hung out with.

Marilyn was the one that Jack was to fall for, however. I could see this and gave up on fighting it within myself. I accepted it, and Jack was happier than I'd ever seen him.

There was a problem shaping up that both Jack and Marilyn couldn't know at first love. This was the religious conflict between two families of O'Conners and Nadlers: Jewish versus Catholic. This was a conflict that has remained insurmountable for thousands of years for thousands of similar relationships, and as the relationships grew so did the religious problem, not between Jack and Marilyn but within the Nadler family. Mixed marriages were not to be, and that was the way it was.

Jack bought a ring for Marilyn and asked her to become engaged, and Marilyn accepted. This was an unbelievable night, and they were both in love with each other.

When the Nadlers discovered what happened and the seriousness of the situation, a meeting was prompted between Jack's parents and Marilyn's parents.

I was there, and I saw how this affected everyone. The sadness of the situation is that they broke up an everlasting love between two people who never forgot each other after they were broken apart. Jack's dad (Dick) and mom (Kay) were also reluctant to do this, but they saw the importance to the Nadlers that Marilyn should marry within her own people.

It was sad but true, and I felt so sorry that Jack had to break it off. This didn't end their friendship or contact with each other, but any idea of marriage was out the window.

With this hanging over them, things were never the same, and the union was never completed.

Jack went on to marry once, and Marilyn, four times.

My love life consisted of a variation. There was the girl, who shall remain nameless, that gave me the first real experience with sex. She was my call girl that I would call up to meet down the street from her place. I didn't want to be seen with her because of reputation. As if that would matter, because my reputation was to become much worse than hers. The stigma of being loose as a girl in those days was taken seriously by all the do-gooders—the people who went to church on Sundays but did not live by the golden rule for the other six days of the week.

These people were the establishment of Gull Lake. They were well-to-do, but sometimes they also had problems that ran deep. But they somehow covered them up enough that no one could prove their wrongs. Nor would you dare for fear of reprisal.

There was the gay druggist, the alcoholic barber, the alcoholic principal's wife, and the pedophile schoolteacher who preyed on students. They were too many for the small town of Gull Lake. But life went on, and no charges were laid, but lives were changed because of the dysfunctional lives of a few.

In fact, I can attest to these people because they interfered in my life. The principal I related to previously had a bitter attitude toward anyone who drank because of his wife's problem. The druggist was to come on to me during a drinking spree thinking I was too drunk to reject his advances. He was oh-so-wrong and wound up down the stairs of his drugstore, where he contemplated what he had done.

The gay grade eight schoolteacher was the most difficult to deal with because I had a lot of respect for him. We drank together and did some deep talking about life and the future.

One night after partying and too much drinking he drove me home and I invited him in to have a drink with Dad, who was up drinking anyway. We went into my house and I had one drink with Dad, Mom, and the teacher.

I was tired and drunk and bored so I went to bed. It was about three o'clock in the morning when I awoke in a state of arousal to discover the teacher's head where it shouldn't be. I jumped out of bed and over him and raced for the door. I tried to get my car started, but the starter was not working. I had left it parked on our small hill coming into our yard, but no way would it start that night of all nights. I walked and ran the two miles to town, where I knew I could stay at Jack's place. I told Jack the next day but only part of the story. I never told anyone else. I was embarrassed, confused, and disappointed. This situation would repeat another time, but for the life of me, I don't know what the attraction was to me. Being poor and drinking is what I analyzed to be the cause and effect.

The barber's problem resulted in a poor haircut many times. He was a character you could tolerate.

There were probably more drunks per capita and area in Gull Lake than anywhere I've ever been since.

This fact led me to believe that my problem with drinking too much was okay. Many of Dad's friends were way too heavy into booze and drinking and would carry on for days at our place.

Our house was a good place for the heavy drinkers and gamblers to come. We were out of town, out of sight of the do-goods, and the party had no ending. Dad welcomed anyone who had a drink with him.

My mom didn't start to drink until everyone except me left home. She was fifty-four then. This was not her cup of tea anyway. She wouldn't get drunk very easily and would fall asleep. It wasn't too long until she would go into deep depression and sit bent over in a chair and staring at the floor for hours.

She lost all ambition and became very unkempt personally, and the house was a mess. This wasn't like her in the past, and I felt sorry for her. I drank to put all of these problems out of my mind, but I was really creating more problems for myself.

Some I couldn't solve: the illegal possession charges I incurred, the undue care and attention from crashing on grad night, and the speeding tickets. The attitude I developed toward the law was not good.

The Shaunavon connection was the bright spot of my teenage years.

They were good people there. The Nadlers, Volls, Olsons, and Ogdens were good, solid citizens. Drinking wasn't that cool with them because they were successful and church meant something besides a cover.

I really like Brenda Olsen, and she just liked me. This was okay with me because I knew she liked to be around the band and we had fun times with her. We hung out together long enough to ask her to graduation when I was an undergrad *twice*!

She was my escort, and I introduced her to my grade eleven teacher, Gerry Norick. They would eventually get married, and I'm happy for them.

However I developed the reputation I was building, and the damage I was doing to myself never affected my relationship with the one girl I respected and who never looked down on me or gave up on me. That girl was Betty Buck.

I didn't appreciate how important she was to me until we met again in Calgary, where she proved how mature she was as a city girl going to school.

These girls at this time held me together as I was coming unwound.

# CHAPTER 13

# Music, Football, and Party Time

With the band rockin' and rollin', the Shaunavon connection, and school in the background, our lives were full.

This was the period when a math teacher by the name of Doug Lyon came to Gull Lake.

The year 1961 was when and Doug was young (twenty-three years old). He was single but was going out with a girl from Swift Current by the name of Deanna Craig, whom he met at Teacher's College.

Still a bachelor, he rented a house that everyone called the Sells House since it was owned by the Sells family. He teamed up with another teacher type by the name of Gerry Elmslie, and they were bachelors in a house with no indoor toilet. The fight was about who would empty the biffy that they had to use in inclement weather. That's about the only fight they ever had. They got along fine, a scheme to draw up plays and make athletes out of boys and girls that only needed direction. There was plenty of talent that needed coaching and guidance. These two young teachers provided that. They were exited to teach, and we were willing to learn.

The year 1961 was a teaching year in football. We played six-man football as the provincial body decided that the towns couldn't support the twelve-man style that the cities played.

Maple Creek was more suited to the six-man game, where the field was open to fast runners. We lost two games to Maple Creek, preventing us from advancing to the provincial playoffs.

Doug Lyon married his fiancée in 1961 and settled in a house with her. This gave Doug more time to concentrate on teaching and coaching.

When 1962 rolled in, I was in track and field. I won through the local track meet in Gull Lake, then on to Swift Current and won there to go to the provincials in Regina. Pole vault, discus, and javelin were my events. I didn't win in Regina, but I was forever linked with Doug Lyon after that and believed in him. My attitude and talent fell short of perfection, but I was in the top 25 percent, in my mind at least. My standing long jump record still stands today. That's as much as I achieved in paper.

I learned a lot from Doug Lyon. I learned sportsmanship, which to me is the quality you learn when you battle with each other but shake hands and congratulate the other and give him the credit he deserves for beating you at a game that was only a game.

The other quality was respect for each other. He taught us to respect each boy or girl that we came into contact with as if they were a member of our family. He called this "the family of life." This remains with me today. As I've gone through life's tough times, I've stayed true to this theme. Everyone has good and bad attributes, sometimes the good is covered up, but I've found it's always there if you look hard enough.

Later on when I would be imprisoned in jail this would prove to be a very useful tool.

The year 1962 was the real deal. Football changed to an eight-man style from six-man. This format provided more strategies because there was more blocking and the game became rougher.

We were fortunate enough to have players that could fulfill the positions. With a small population to choose from, it was incredible to have this kind of talent.

Doug Lyon saw this and applied his knowledge of the game to the players available.

One of the players was Barry Aldag. He was built like a bull, and all two hundred and thirty pounds of him was muscle. He was a farm boy of the best stock. He played center on both offence and defense and he could advance a team on his back or stop a team from advancing. Doug Lyon would tell him what to do and Barry would get it done. Barry would eventually move on to the Saskatchewan Roughriders for three years playing in the CFL.

Barry's brother, Roger, would follow, and Roger would be part of the Grey Cup winners of Saskatchewan. Eventually in 1989, Roger would be inducted into the Football Hall of Fame.

Another star player of the Gull Lake Lion Football team (The name *Lions* was decided upon while Doug Lyon was coaching to pay tribute to the man who made it all happen) was Darryl Lloyd. He was six foot three, weighed two hundred pounds, and was very good looking. He was the leader of the team.

He set records for yardage, touchdowns, and pass receptions, and he was key to our team.

There were many others such as Fred Homann, guard and tackle. Ron Schoneck, quarterback, who cried when we were losing, as he was unbelievably competitive. There was Lenny Hay, who could tackle with only his fingertips outstretched. Jack, my buddy, was another strong player playing halfback

I was in defense mostly, but I was also teamed up with Lenny Hay to return punts and kickoffs. We would complement each other in this suicidal task, and we loved it. This was tragic for me in one of the games I'll explain in detail soon.

The year 1962 was the beginning of eight-man football, but we still couldn't beat Maple Creek to advance to the provincials. They were strong and fast, and we were close but not quite good enough.

The year 1963 was when Gull Lake would become known across the province for its football. This was the beginning of eighteen years of league championships and a dynasty of winning football teams. It was a record of over two hundred wins and thirty-six losses over eighteen years under Gerry Elmslie, who replaced Doug Lyon when Doug moved on to Melfort, Saskatchewan to run their program. This culminated in eight provincial championships for Gull Lake, which tells the story of how successful Doug Lyon and Gerry Elmslie made the players from the smallest town in all of competitive eight-man and nine-man high school football in Canada.

Gerry has passed on, but Doug still lives in Melfort, Saskatchewan.

In 1963, we got our taste of success. We won the Southwest League undefeated and moved to provincial play defeating the much bigger town of Assiniboia to advance to the finals in Meadow Lake, Saskatchewan. Meadow Lake was a long, long way from Gull Lake. This was quite an undertaking for a small team to take on. Transportation was not as accessible then. We went by cars to Meadow Lake and took time off school. This was cool with us, but our fans were few. Not too many fans had the resources to travel that far.

We were billeted in homes in Meadow Lake. Jack and I stayed in the same place. We didn't realize it at that time, but the home was of the player who would beat us single-handedly in the final game. Twenty-four to seventeen was the score, and we were very downhearted in the return trip back to Gull Lake.

Although we had lost, we had gone further than any football team from Gull Lake before us. For this we were heroes. We would get crowds up to a thousand people. They would surround the football field with cars and pickups, and people would stand around the field cheering and clapping.

The year 1964 was thought to be the year of the provincial championship for the Gull Lake Lions. The semifinals brought North Battleford Mustangs to town. The cars circled the football field, and the scene was set for the big game.

We ran onto the field with the entire crowd behind us. We were intimidating to the bigger team of North Battleford in the fact that we had so much support.

As the game progressed, I was returning a punt. I gathered the ball up deep in our end and headed up field trying to pick up blocking. I was too deep behind our blockers when four tacklers came deep to hit me. I withstood the first tackler, but the next three piled on. My leg snapped under their weight against my spikes. My ankle shattered, and I went down in severe pain. I screamed in agony, and everyone heard the pain. They carted me off to the hospital in a stretcher, and I was given a shot of morphine.

My sister Lois, (the oldest) a nurse, and another nurse by the name of Agnes McTaggert were my angels of mercy for a couple of days. They decided that there was nothing they could do for me in Gull Lake, so they sent me to Regina to be operated on. I was tended to by a Dr. Bachinski, who was a specialist in bad breaks. He inserted a screw to hold my ankle together, and after two weeks in Regina General Hospital, I went back to Gull Lake on crutches. For six months I was a worried young man. I was told then that I would have a limp for the rest of my life and that there was nothing more that could be done for me.

One thing was said though that I listened to very carefully. The doctor said that when the cast comes off, walking in sand would be good therapy. I did a lot of walking in sand, and I do not have a limp and feel no repercussions from the break. I still have the screw, and for years the airport security used to pick up the steel in my leg. This would cause great concern in airports from time to time.

To me it was a badge of honor because I'll never forget the day I broke my ankle and why.

The girlfriend I had at that game against North Battleford was Julie Houston from Shaunavon. She was cute and popular, and I was proud to have her there. She wasn't prepared to go to the hospital, however. I felt bad for her, but shit happens, and I had a lot of visitors while I was in the hospital in Gull Lake. Julie was the daughter of a butcher and the sister of a dentist, so I guess she had seen lots of pain before.

Regina Hospital was a different story. I was transported on a station wagon for 185 miles by a guy named Chip Sweeting. He was very helpful and kind. He did this for nothing, and I will always be grateful.

The two weeks in Regina I spent on my own. I met some good people, but I was terribly lonely and scared.

Going home was wonderful, and I remember that my sister and her husband came to get me.

The game against North Battleford ended up 50-8 for Gull Lake. I was told that this game was won because they were going to win it for me. The quarterback for North Battleford also ended up in the hospital bed beside me that day with a broken wrist, so that was some comfort to me. He was in more pain than I was because I was already on a morphine trip when he arrived.

# CHAPTER 14

## Sex, Football, and Music

Somewhere in this maze of events, we had time for the inevitable sex, booze, and cars. Cars were easy: we would buy a piece of junk or borrow Jack's dad's or my dad's pickup. We always had wheels to get us from A to B.

We became experts at making things run. Gas money was sometimes a problem, but we managed to pitch in together to fill up.

I got my driver's license in January 1962 when the weather was brutal. I borrowed Jack's dad's car. It was a black '55 Ford with a police light on top. I guess the driver examiner was impressed because I got 100 percent on the exam. Right on. I was very excited that I took the car back to Jack's, went home to get Dad's pickup, and never went to pick up Jack. He was pissed about that and still reminds me today of this little slight.

I was wrapped up in the power of driving. The freedom to go anywhere was empowering. This feeling was to get me into a lot of trouble down the road, however.

Even when I broke my ankle, I could drive. This was when girls became so important to me. They were status symbols for us boys in the sixties.

Any girl that was prone to having sex before marriage was like a magnet to a piece of steel.

One particular girl who shall remain unnamed was special to me. She was babysitting one night, and Jack, Gerry Moore, and I all went to visit. She and I went to the bedroom, and my virginity was lost that night. Jack and Gerry were on the other side of the walls. I was in complete ecstasy because not only was I going where I'd never gone before, I was there before them.

Such was the loss of innocence, and the timing was perfect. The song playing on the little radio in the room was "Rhythm of the Falling Rain." It was a night never to forget and a song to remember.

There were a few girls around like her, but never to repeat that experience.

As I went through school and the teenage years, I developed a bad reputation. Not too many fathers would allow their daughters to go out with me. If I did succeed in dating someone from Gull Lake I would have to drop them off well before their house so that their dad wouldn't see who they were with.

This was not the case with one particular girl by the name of Betty Buck. She was blonde, nice looking, and smart. We conversed a lot and got along well. She would be whom I could take to any function or place to have a date. She was willing and able to go anywhere and never turn me down. She wasn't into sex, and she wasn't about to give herself up. This I understood, but I liked her a lot. She was a free spirit and an independent thinker.

She became the girlfriend of our drummer, Gerry Voll, but other than that, she didn't give herself to anyone for keeps until she moved to Calgary and got married.

We traveled many miles playing in our band. We would use Jack's dad's police car sometimes, sometimes Ed Cunningham's white '58 Chevy Impala, a two-door hardtop. One time we were going to play for a dance at White Bear, Saskatchewan. A grad. Dance at that. So all the kids were waiting for us to get there.

When we crossed the South Saskatchewan River north of Swift Current, the river was breaking up and the ferry wasn't running. The ice had re-formed on the river so there was a layer of ice with two feet of water under the ice, and then there was the main ice underneath. We probably shouldn't have crossed, but the dance was waiting to happen so we crossed anyway. The upper ice broke, and we were spinning out. Ed stayed in to drive, I was in the back with my leg in a cast, and Jack and Jim Steadman were pushing. We got across, and we were only one hour late. The crowd cheered, and we had a great night.

Another memorable dance we played was at our own Elks Hall. This was the stage where we loved to play. The sound was excellent, and we were at the far end facing the entrance, where we could see the crowd coming in. By watching who was coming in, we could tell what kind of crowd we were going to have. In those days, the classes of people dictated the who's who and where they were going.

This dance was like no other we had before. The crowd kept coming in until the hall was full. The night was warm and the atmosphere was hot. It was fall, and football was the game of the season.

Before the dance, we picked up four dozens of beer to party with after the dance. We had Jack's dad's car. He had traded off his black '55 Ford for a '57 Ford and hadn't installed the light on top yet. We had our beer in the backseat and felt pretty secure with the car parked in the back of the hall along the alley.

The dance progressed, and the mood was intense. A few fights broke out, and Jack was involved in one of them. A bitter Dean Dixon from Shaunavon was in love with Marilyn, Jack's girlfriend. Dean approached the stage and wanted to fight. Jack was not confrontational; he didn't want trouble to break out. But the angry Dixon wouldn't let up. Jack jumped off the stage, grabbed him by the throat, and forced him out the side door. "Outside, asshole," was all Jack said. The fight was on, and Jack had him down on the sidewalk and hit him, but Dixon wouldn't quit. A fellow by the name of Jack Saum grabbed Jack by the shoulders in an arm lock and pulled Jack off. To this day, I swear, Jack would have killed this jealous Dean Dixon, but luckily, he went back to Shaunavon beaten and bruised, and he vowed for revenge later.

After the dance was over, we packed up our gear and headed to Jack's dad's car. Beer was foremost on our minds at this point. However, there wasn't any in the backseat. "Son of a bitch!" We exclaimed in unison. Somebody stole it, but how? The car was locked, and everyone in town knew it was the town cop's car. But the beer was gone and we were pissed off. No bootleggers were around at that time and the bar was closed.

We had a dry night, and partying was short that night. Off we went to Jack's house to lament and discuss the night.

When we arrived at Jack's, there were two cases of twenty-four beers sitting on the floor at the door. These were the cases that we had in the cop's car at the dance. We knew we were in trouble, because we were all under age.

Jack's dad had a spare key and checked his car out and found the beer. Lyle Fostier, the young aggressive RCMP that Dick was riding with that night thought that taking our beer would screw up our night, and he was right. Lyle was a very, very good detective, and he could figure out where we were going drinking before we even got there. He went on to be an undercover drug detective in Vancouver and was instrumental in busting a lot of big drug deals on the West Coast.

We all stayed over at Jack's house that night. In the morning, Dick yelled up the stairs, and we knew we were in deep shit.

We all sat around the table while Dick and Lyle gave us an ultimatum. "You guys can decide who is going to take the ticket for illegal possession of this booze, or we will charge all of you. We'll go to the restaurant for breakfast, and when we get back, someone or everyone will be charged."

We sat looking at each other after they left. We looked at the beer and looked at each other until I grabbed a beer and popped the top. Everyone else did the same. We drank every bottle and put the empties back in the boxes where they came in.

We left the house, and Dick and Lyle came back home to discover what we had done.

No evidence, no charge. We got away with that one more out of humor than justice.

We put one over on the two best cops Gull Lake ever had, since before. There were more serious events that will happen with the law, but this one was funny.

# CHAPTER 15

# Changes, Music, and Drinking

Gerry Voll was our drummer, but it was sometimes awkward because Gerry lived in Shaunavon, which was thirty-two miles away. And when we needed to practice, Gerry usually wasn't there. This would introduce a back-up drummer by the name of Jim Steadman. His dad owned the GM dealership in Gull Lake. *Jim* was also his dad's name, and he was your typical high-powered salesman. This gave us two things: cars and a drummer.

Jim was previously from Swift Current, and he was mature beyond his years. He was fast-talking, cool with women, and was a natural drummer. He provided us with the new beat of the Stones and the Animals on the drums, and the music was different in a way that made us feel like we had discovered a new sound.

Jim also had a complete set of drums.

Gerry and I decided to get very drunk one night, and the night turned into day, but we didn't quit. We had a dance to play in Antelope, where we had played before. The dances at that hall were good because that's all there was there—a dance hall—no store, no hotel, and most importantly, no cops. Antelope was only six miles east of Gull Lake, but the cops didn't usually show up unless they were called.

Two things resulted from that drinking binge: I couldn't play guitar because I was drunk, and Gerry was very uncoordinated. He ended up falling into his drums, and the dance was over. Jack was very pissed, and we thought the band was over.

I talked my way around this scene, but Gerry was finished. Enter Jim Steadman. He took over the drums, and we carried on.

Jim fit in very well. He also fit in with the Shaunavon girl scene. He could talk a girl into doing things that she wouldn't ordinarily do with anyone else.

He had a creative side, and there was no better way to show creativeness than music. He had excellent ideas for the band. We had changed our name to the Jack and the Rippers using the Jack the Ripper name from the murderous villain from London, England.

Jim suggested a classier name for the band, so we changed it to the Coachmen.

Our equipment—guitars, amplifiers, PA system, and drums—were of much better quality, and our selection of music, more complex.

This was where Jack's and Jim's personalities collided. Both were born leaders, but Jim was quick and fast-witted. This would piss Jack off, and the relationship among us all suffered.

Eventually we were destined to fall apart. Jack keeps playing to this day, and Ed Cunningham has a studio at the basement of his home in Regina, where he records music. I play from time to time, but only when the feeling to make painful music on the guitar arises because my fingers aren't in shape.

We would play so much that we had no fingerprints showing from the calluses that were formed from pressing on the strings.

Jim Steadman meant a lot to me. He had a perceptive mind, and I needed that at that time. Whether it was a girl problem, a family problem, or a music problem, Jim was there to talk to, provide insight, and give me support. He never criticized, but somehow he gave me the thought that maybe I could turn things around by looking within myself.

He was a live for today person in the first degree. He personified the song, "Live For Today."

He was into cars, motors, and how an automobile should look and perform.

He would get me into my first new car soon after I left Gull Lake, Saskatchewan, for the rich oilfields of Alberta.

# CHAPTER 16

## Oil, Money, and More Booze

The year 1965 was a turning point for me. I finished school three subjects short of graduating from grade twelve. I was one year back after failing grade eleven. So I was an undergrad, but I attended graduation anyway as such.

I drank way too much that night. Orange gin and vodka weren't quite what I needed, but I became very drunk. I drove my two-door 1956 Chev hardtop that I had spent many hours changing motors from a six cylinder to a V8. I was driving this vehicle too fast down highway 37 going through Gull Lake toward the #1 highway. I was going too fast to make the gentle curve before the railway tracks and lost control of the powerful car. I hit the signal light pole head on. The damage was heavy, and I was knocked unconscious and bled from the mouth and nose after my head hit the steering wheel. I woke up with Lyle, the young cop, saying, "Ronnie, are you awake?" through the window. I did wake up and said, "Fuck off!"

He took me out of the car, which by this time was surrounded by bystanders, and the train was stopped before the crossing and waited for the scene to clear.

There were flashing police lights, train lights, and the signal lights for the crossing.

I was loaded into Lyle's police car and taken to the hospital. My sister Lois, and Dr. Ko decided that if I needed a blood test for alcohol, they weren't doing it, so Lyle was perplexed. I wasn't checked out for injuries and reloaded into the police car, which Lyle drove very fast to Swift Current to get a blood test for alcohol to charge me.

Halfway to Swift Current he said, "Well, you can admit that you were drunk and we'll get a written confession so that we won't have to go all the way to Swift Current!"

I said, "Well, Lyle, I don't really care what you will do, but I am not giving you fuck all."

Lyle got extremely mad and turned around in a squealing cop U-turn to take me home to my farm. I went in bleeding, and my mom was very scared. I just went to bed for a while and slept it off.

I was so hung over the next day I could have died, but I walked to town to check out my car. I was remorseful, regretful, and empty while I surveyed the damages.

Dick O'Connor, came along, put his hand on my shoulder, and said, "Ronnie, I just feel sorry for you." That was it. I'll never forget those words.

After graduation, I went through the motions of school, but I didn't care. I finished in June but not the way I wanted to.

I took a clerical position at the Co-op Lumber, a hardware store in Gull Lake. The band was finished, my car was wrecked, and I was broke. I started out at $192 a month, which was hardly enough for the debts I owed, let alone to make a living.

Terry Smart was in Alberta working with seismographs and searching for the elusive oil and gas buried deep under the ground surfaces. Stretching through British Columbia, Alberta, and Saskatchewan.

This was exciting to me too. The more Terry talked about his adventuresome life the more I wanted to be part of it.

Finally, on December 5, 1965, I loaded my meager belongings into Terry's 1966 Caliente Ford convertible and away we went.

But this was not before my dad vented his anger on me, told me that I was good for nothing, and would always be a good-for-nothing son of a bitch. I cried and left with much bitterness and resentment toward him, Gull Lake, and everything that my nineteen years had ever lived through.

We headed west and reached Piapot, where we could get into the bar underage and pick up a case of beer for the long road to Calgary. This was where I discovered I had forgotten my wallet at the farm.

Back we went, and the ugly scene with my dad was repeated.

Oh yes, I'll forever remember this part of my life and the speech Principal Ernie Franks gave to me when he was choking me. These were to be the main catalysts of my life when things got tough. I was forever proving them wrong, and there has never been enough success in my life.

There is a physiological term for this, but I'm not sure what it is. Someone is bound to be able to help me out on that one.

Calgary was beckoning for many of us at that point of time. It was still a small town city then and had all the signs of growth. The sixties was exciting anyway, and we were part of a booming economy.

The Banff Oil/Rainbow Lake discovery was just beginning, and the company Terry and I worked for was Seismotech 64 Ltd. formed by a man by the name of Hal Godwin.

He was a very smooth, shrewd businessman, and he had access to money that was needed to get anywhere in the fast-moving, ever-changing world of seismic.

This was where instrumentation and exploration merged into finding energy deposits by sound amplification generated by dynamites.

I began as a jug hustler. This was the job lowest on the totem pole. The rookie was the jug hustler. I loved to work, however, so consequently I became the best jug hustler. I was made into the boss, which was the line truck driver, who was in-charge of the jug hustlers. We spread the geophones on the ground to pick up the sound when the dynamite was exploded to transfer the sound into the recording instruments of the recording truck that was loaded with computers and translated from instruments to paper all the data from the bowels of the earth and back to the surface.

As we traveled north to Rainbow Lake, a shooter (the man who handles the dynamite) by the name of Ed Schindler was driving in our convoy of trucks. We hit black ice at Whitecourt, and Ed lost control. The truck, a three-ton Chev, went into a skid and rolled. The dynamite flew out of the truck but didn't explode. Without a cap inserted into a stick of a dynamite, it is pretty safe. I didn't know that at that time, so this was a pretty scary scene.

We cut Ed out of the truck, and he spent a little time in the hospital, but he joined us later.

Ed was originally from Gull Lake, I found out later. This proved to be a positive thing for me, as he was tough on men, and we got along fine. Ed was following a tough path in life; he was heavy into booze, hookers, and drugs. His only safe haven was the oilfield camps of the north, where the camps forbid booze and drugs. This was a dry-out period for Ed.

He was brilliant but stopped at shooting in advancement of a career, where he could have easily become a party manager.

He was a free spirit and was easily sucked into the booze when the opportunity arose.

Terry was into surveying and loved it.

I eventually became a shooter, and I loved that job like no other job I had before or since.

I got all the licenses I could get and achieved all the certificates I needed for the future.

---

63

Rainbow Lake was phenomenal. There were ninety eight seismic crews and over one hundred drilling rigs between Rainbow Lake and Zama Lake in 1966.

There were seismic lines criss-crossing, and sometimes lines were cut to allow movement. There were cats directed to travel along the seismic lines and geophones, which ended up in four-inch pieces for up to a mile. It was serious stuff, but there was serious money involved.

We shot Banff Oil, whose shares went from pennies to over twenty dollars a share within a year.

The year 1966 saw us in a camp at Rainbow Lake with 3,500 men until our smaller camp was set up. Here was a camp full of men with one thing on their mind—money. This drove everyone to work in the extreme cold of the north.

Surveyors and cat skinners went where no man had gone before in search of the oil that Rainbow Lake had. And oil there was. Many wells hit 3,000 barrels per day, and life was good.

The big drawback was the proximity to civilization. It was a long way home. We would fly back and forth in a Banff Oil-owned DC3 that they had recovered from Rainbow Lake after it had crashed. They rebuilt the indestructible DC3 and used it for their company. We loved that plane, and the pilots were bush-trained and second to none.

These were exciting times for many men, and money was no object. We made good money because we put in lots of hours. I started at 85¢ per hour, and within four months, I was at a $1.15 an hour.

Our money was in the bank when we finished the winter. This was good and bad. When we would come out with a few thousand dollars in the bank, we would spend all of it and then some during spring breakup, mostly in Calgary, and traveling back to Saskatchewan, where most of us came from.

All the farm boys from the prairies were important to the Alberta oil patch because they were good workers and were trusted.

The American part of the equation was frustrating. These people were engineers, geophysicists, and technicians from Houston, Corpus Christie, and West Texas. They had a hard time with the cold climate, and we used to laugh at them. However, they were experienced and helped us sort out the mysteries that needed to be solved to find the oil and gas of the huge tracts of land we explored.

Some of the days hit sixty degrees below zero Fahrenheit, without wind. We had the newest equipment, but even so, they wouldn't start if we ever shut them off for long.

Tires were flat-bottomed and stayed that way all day while we were driving over the rough tundra that was frozen-solid on top. But if you were unlucky and broke through, the muskeg became a quicksand and sucked anything that fell through out of sight. Many trucks, cats, and even rigs were swallowed up by the muskeg, which had no bottom. A lot of equipment was salvaged by companies that specialized in the recovery of lost equipment. They made a lot of money because an oil change a clean up, and the equipment was like new to be sold for top dollar. A lot of these people were from Edmonton, and they thrived in this endeavor.

We explored Rainbow, Zama Lake, Fort St. John, Fort Nelson, Pointed Mountain, Red Earth, Fort Vermillion, and High Prairie. These were some in that vast expanse of territory.

Summer time was easy for us. We would be sent to Saskatchewan and Eastern Alberta to shoot and map out areas where the geologists for the big oil companies figured the would-be deposits. Without us, they could only wildcat-drill. It was a higher percentage after we shot the area.

The winter of 1969 I moved on from Seismotech to Teledyne Industries. They were bigger and American-owned. They needed a shooter, and I fit the bill for them at that time.

I started, and we went to Fort Nelson, plus one hundred miles east to Pointed Mountain. This was a severe terrain, and this was also the famous Liard River. Twelve prospectors had been found in the area with no heads, so the name Headless Valley became the stuff of legends.

We were camped in the middle, and there was a spooky feeling about the area. There were hot springs in the midst of a forty-below weather. There were willows and trees greened up because of the hot springs, and we had never experienced anything like this before.

Our party manager was a hard-nosed, fiery man by the name of Ed Gates. He was one of the hardest party managers to ever head up a crew.

He was tough, but he wanted results. He understood every facet about seismograph; thereby, nothing got by him.

He would call you on anything that he didn't think was right. I was his shooter, he liked me, and I worked my ass off for him.

During this time in Pointed Mountain, I met a man by the name of Harvey Watson. He owned an air\water drilling rig combination. This was the rig that we used to drill through the hard rock of Pointed Mountain to drop the dynamite from 40 feet to 120 feet, depending on where they wanted the shot to start.

We were loading twenty to forty pounds of dynamite, and I was preloading as soon as the rigs drilled the holes. I met Harvey while doing this. He was full of hot temper, and he and Ed Gates locked horns many times. They hated each other, but Ed needed Harvey because Harvey could drill and he had the only rig that could drill through rocks.

There was a mountain ridge separating our camps from the field we were drilling out, so Ed asked me if I could open up a road to get there instead of having to drive two hours each day around it.

We went out and drilled some shot holes. I loaded the dynamite, and we blew a pass through. We shortened our days, and everyone was happy.

Harvey got stuck with his rig in a soft spot created by a hot spring so I went out with him and his helper one night in Harvey's pickup.

I told them the story about when I went to visit my sister the spring before in Toronto. I went on and on about a girl that I had a blind date with, and when I went to pick her up, she had no legs and was in a wheelchair. We went out anyway, and I put her wheelchair in the trunk of my car. We went to a drive-in movie and then I took her home. On the way to her house she started talking about having sex and that she always fantasized about it. I got into this with her, and she said she had straps in her wheelchair and that if I wanted, I could strap her arms, hang her from a tree, and make love to her.

Harvey and his helper were totally engrossed in the story. I carried on to tell explicitly how this was done. Then I said I took her home and took the wheelchair and her to her door, where her dad met us and thanked me. He then came after me and gave me ten dollars. I said, "What's this for?"

He replied, "All the other guys left her hanging on the tree, and I'd have to send a cab to get her. So I may as well give you the money."

Well this was just about suicide when they found out it was a joke. Harvey to this day will never forget that night, and we are still friends.

That spring when we returned to Calgary, Ed Gates asked me if I wanted to change careers from being a shooter to becoming a Vibroseis operator. I said, "Sure, Ed." I knew they were headed to Wyoming and Louisiana because I had met some of his crew. Ed said to go and take a couple of weeks and visit whomever because I wouldn't be back to Alberta for three years.

Off I went to Gull Lake, of course. At this time, Jim Steadman and Jack O'Connor, my old band buddies, were into bikes. They belonged to a gang in Swift Current called the Spokesmen. This was great. It was just what I needed: drinking, drugs, and lots of women. I had no control of any of this action. I just enjoyed every sin there that happened to be at the moment.

I overindulged and ended up losing my license for three months, which ended my career as a Vibroseis operator. Instead, I ended up in Nordegg, Alberta, running a Nodwell-tracked vehicle in the most godforsaken country seismograph was ever performed in my experience.

The car I was driving was sold to me by Jim Steadman in Gull Lake. This was a midnight blue 1969 Firebird with a 350-cubic inch 325 HP and three-speed standard transmission. This was all stock, and that car would have flown if it had wings. At 160 miles per hour on the speedometer, I took it all the way several times. This was the car that I was driving when I got stopped for drunk-driving. They only stopped me by roadblock because they couldn't catch me.

A three-month suspension was light, but that was what I got. This suspension was only in Saskatchewan, and I was able to drive in Alberta. However, this gave me a record that wouldn't allow me across the United States border.

This car was my status symbol. It was my chick magnet, and I loved it. In two short years, I put 40,000 miles on it, with most of the miles in the summer months.

# CHAPTER 17

## Pursuing Other Careers and Trying to Settle Down

Each spring we were laid off for a while for spring breakup. After month of work and saving money, we were ready. We were like racehorses coming out of the chute. We'd congregate in Calgary, and the favorite motel to stay at was the Continental Motel on Macleod Trail. Here was where the seismograph crews made home while their money lasted. This was usually only a month because the bars and the cabarets beckoned, and we were the most willing customers.

The characters of this time were unforgettable. There was Doc Wiggins, who was one of the funniest people I'd ever met. There was John Hofer, an ex-Hutterite from southern Alberta who tested everyone he met by fighting with them. He could do pushups with one hand with two people sitting on his back. He had no enemies, and it took nine cops to get him into jail in Calgary, one fight-filled night.

We used to go into the Trade Winds Hotel around lunchtime with all intentions of going back to Teledyne's shop to fix trucks, but noon turned to two o'clock in the morning at the cabaret, where drinking was allowed if you brought your own bottle and bought a two-dollar mix. Under-the-table clubs, they were called "live entertainment," and there were many women to dance with.

We would sit down at a table and tell the waitress to "bring a hundred and call the cops."

This was sometimes to become fact, as we created trouble that sometimes the cops could only handle late in the night.

---

During the spring of 1970 I went to Gull Lake. Jack was preparing to move with his boss Tony Mulders, who had a plumbing and heating business in Gull Lake. He was moving to Kelowna, British Columbia, and Jack was agonizing over moving. But he was apprenticing as a plumber, so in order to pursue his trade, he pretty well had to go with Tony.

I helped Jack move to British Columbia and took my '69 Firebird. Jack had a '69 El Camino that he loved. Off we went, and Kelowna was awesome. I fell in love with the city and fell in love with a girl named Darlene Brown. She made the song, Mrs. Brown you have a Lovely Daughter, come to life for me.

She was heavy on the hips, but she was smart and manipulative. I didn't realize the last part until it was too late, but I liked her enough to ask her to marry me with the ring and everything. She accepted, but it didn't last.

Her parents talked her out of this relationship. Another situation developed that definitely ended this also. Jack was seduced by this same lovely daughter of Mrs. Brown, and when he told me this, I was destroyed.

When we went to Kelowna, we were looking for something to do other than just party on the beach and drink. We spotted some ball players practicing at Elks Stadium in Kelowna. We had our ball gloves with us, so we played catch off to the side because they looked way too serious to approach.

We were playing catch when the coach of the senior baseball team approached us and asked if we wanted to join them.

We did, and being pretty good ball players, we were asked to try out. I loved baseball and played lots of it in Gull Lake. Jack was a good hitter, and I was a fairly good pitcher. We both made the team, and this began a two-year spring summer thing for me.

The first year was the Kelowna Carlings, the second, Kelowna Labatts. As you can tell, we were sponsored by the breweries of the day. They supplied the beer, the uniforms, and some expense money.

We played, and the team found jobs for anyone needing a job.

More than half the team were from the States, colleges, castoffs from pro teams, or players that were injured but were rehabilitating. One of these rehabs was Jerry Robinson. He was signed with the Kansas City Royals. He was as black as coal, and he could hit big time. When he would, the ball would hit the sweet spot of the bat, and that ball would disappear into the nightlights and into the black sky. Some balls that he would hit would travel more than 400 feet. Another player worth mentioning here was Don Rogilstadt, who went on to the New York Yankees.

Our league included Kamloops, Penticton, Trail, and Grand Forks, and we played in the Lacombe tournament each year.

Our manager-owner was connected with Idaho, Oregon, California, and Nevada. We were always flush with talent, but then so were the other teams.

We would easily draw 1,000-1,500 people in some games.

I was alive, and I relished the pitching starts I got. My hitting sucked, but I had some good games pitching.

When the big split between Darlene and me happened, I quit the team and went to Nelson, British Columbia, where my brother worked. Malcolm and his wife Rosalie were solid, and thought I was pretty wild. They were right, and I tried not to act up too much around them.

After I left Kelowna for Nelson, I stopped in at Grand Forks to see the playing manager of their baseball team. He suggested I play for them. I was right into that, as I knew they played against Kelowna. There was one interlocking game left to play between Kelowna and Grand Forks, so I wanted to be part of it.

It took two weeks to get a release from Kelowna in writing. They tried to extend this time so that I couldn't play the game coming up, but Grand Forks pushed them.

I was hired by the hotel in Grand Forks as a bartender/waiter. I was good at waiting on tables, but I had a hard time breaking up fights without getting into the middle myself.

There were many Doukabor people in Grand Forks, and a lot of them were related to each other. This was where you had to be careful as to how you treated them, because they could all turn against you if you were the outsider.

One of these was a pretty girl, who was a single mother. She was what I needed coming off a bitter love affair in Kelowna.

We proceeded to play baseball in Grand Forks, and we played against Rosie Baird of the famous Queen and her court team of only five. They would take on any team, and out of all the games they played to that time, they only lost four across Canada and the United States.

Rosie could throw underhand at 105 miles per hour, and for a trick, she would pitch from second base and strike batters out.

Grand Forks was the one team that had beaten them, so this year was a rematch. We lost 7-4, but they only played with us like toys on a string. They were fabulous. Rosie was gorgeous. They were also managed by their father, who was into evangelism. They were promoting religion with fastball, and it worked for them.

We tried dating them, but this was to no avail. Their father was all over that.

I made the trip to Kelowna by myself two days before the big game. I took my Firebird and headed out. I was pumped because I was going to pitch against my old team.

When I arrived in Kelowna, I picked up Jack and we went out. Brent Gloekler and some buddies of his were staying in a rat hole apartment on

Rutland Road. We partied there until the subject of Darlene Brown came up. This evolved into the only fight Jack and I ever had. He was reluctant to fight, and most of the fight he spent pushing me back. But I wouldn't quit, and eventually I hit him in the throat, damaging his wind pipe, and I had two broken ribs.

I was hurt, but I wasn't telling anyone. I had a game to pitch. I would have to be dead to miss this. The next day I bandaged up tight and applied lots of Heet liniment to mask the pain.

The game began, and I was pitching. The crowd was big, and the paper played the situation pretty good. The crowd hated me and let me know, and I relished in the hate.

I pitched all nine innings, and we lost 7-4, but there were seven errors behind me. We could have won, but, oh well, I got to strike out the big homerun hitter Jerry Robinson three times, so I was happy.

I returned to Grand Forks two days after. I was hurt, broke, disillusioned, and depressed.

When I got back, I discovered that the transmission was going out of my Firebird. This prompted a choice I had to make: either fix it and pay for it with money I didn't have or trade it off for a Mercury Marauder for only a $2,300 difference, money that I also didn't have.

I went to the bank to arrange a loan, but I needed a cosigner. I phoned my brother in Nelson.

"Malcolm," I said, "will you cosign for me until I get back to Alberta and go to work?"

"I don't know. I will have to talk to Rosalie about that," replied Malcolm. I was so sure he would do it that I went ahead and wrote the check. They released the car, but my brother didn't cosign, and the check was bound to bounce.

I knew this was going to happen, so I headed south to the States, where I kept driving until my money ran out.

I was stranded in Wenatchee, Washington, when I just gave myself up to a sheriff. He asked what I had done, and all I said was, "You're the detective. You find out."

They took me back to British Columbia and handed me over to the RCMP. The RCMP took me to Grand Forks, where charges were pressed for uttering false pretenses, and I was charged, convicted, and sentenced to four months in jail. I was taken to Penticton for trial, to Kamloops to jail, and then to Wells Grey Forestry Camp to do the time.

This was the most depressing, distressing time I had ever been through, and I was torn apart. I knew that I had reached bottom but only wanted to get out and go to work again.

Every waking moment with the lazy, useless people I met in jail made me want to change my way of life.

I didn't want any part of this life.

I put on a lot of weight in jail. I was up to 190 pounds when I got out, which was twenty pounds over my weight. I was sluggish and lazy.

I was released in September. I was given a free room by the Salvation Army for one night, and the next day I was on a Greyhound free pass to Nelson, British Columbia to stay with my brother Malcolm. No regrets, just happiness that I was free.

From Nelson, Malcolm drove me back to Calgary, where I stayed with my sister Vangie and her husband, Rudy, who let me stay until I reapplied for a job with Teledyne.

My brother Orville came up from Swift Current, and the four of us went to Forest Lawn Hotel on a Saturday for beer. We sat around a table and Rudy asked me how I was for money. I said I had two dollars that Mom had sent me. We laughed about that, and Rudy slipped me twenty dollars. I'll never forget that help. I paid him back, but I sure needed that support more mentally than financially.

# CHAPTER 18

## A Hill to Climb

I was fortunate to be able to go to Teledyne to get my job back. They accepted me without questioning about where I'd been, and I kept my secret from them.

They had my job record on file so I just carried on like I hadn't been away. I was sent to Foothills South, which is west of Calgary in the Sheep River Mountains. They were shooting a refraction project that required a shooter. This particular job was more than I had ever tackled before. One shot per day, which was 2,000 lbs of dynamite all loaded in the same hole.

Every day I thought about killing myself because I was depressed and I was at an end. But every day I returned to camp, and every day I got stronger. Mentally I was torn apart, but deep down inside I had enough left to carry on.

After the first couple of checks from Teledyne, I felt much better.

A guy by the name of Julian Nerada was on this job with me. He was to become a buddy, and he had a nice '70 Mustang.

We traveled together, and we would go to Calgary to the bar scene and arrive back at camp just in time for work.

We moved from that project to Chain Lakes to finish the project, but while tripping back and forth to Calgary, we were in the Trade Winds Hotel when one noon hour we were doing shop time and we watched some secretaries come in. One of these was Sharon Beres. I didn't meet them at noon, but I watched as they walked in. Julian and a couple other guys invited them back when they got off work.

Sure enough, at five o'clock they were back, but our table was full of people and booze. Sharon was standing beside my chair, and I said, "sit here," pointing to my leg. So she did sit on my lap, and I talked, drank, and flirted with her.

By this time our work detail at Chain Lakes was over and we were back staying in the motel. This time, however, the Continental Motel was full, so I took a room in a log cabin-type motel south of Macleod Trail.

This was okay because I partied at the Continental and slept at my log cabin.

I met Sharon and partied with her, and got to like her. However there was another girl on the scene already that I didn't have the heart to get rid of right away.

This overlap almost ended the relationship Sharon and I had began.

I was not into a serious relationship and had no intention of repeating the mistake I had made in Kelowna, British Columbia.

I was asked by Teledyne to go to Rocky Mountain House on a Nodwell camp job for a few weeks. I went and asked Sharon to store my meager belongings, which consisted of a guitar, some clothes, and memorabilia I had.

She agreed, and off I went to a job in the Foothills, west of Rocky Mountain House, which I hated, but I needed the cash.

When we finished the job, I went back to Calgary to find out there would be a layoff as the work had fallen off. This was okay by me; I was ready for a change.

Little did I realize how much of a change.

I suggested to Sharon that she should maybe quit her job at Comines Fertilizer in Calgary and we should go to Vancouver. She was reluctant at first, but the more exciting I made it sound, the more inviting the suggestion became.

She was engaged to a boy from Lestock, Saskatchewan, where she was from, and had the rings.

We left Calgary in her Vauxhall Viva car, which had four cylinders and was very uncomfortable from what I was used to driving.

I didn't have a vehicle, and I kept pretty closemouthed about her car.

We left Calgary for the mountains. Sharon had never been to British Columbia before, so this was a new experience for her. We arrived in Kelowna with this little car and met up with Jack, who by then was married to a girl by the maiden name of Doreen Hamel. As it turned out, Doreen and Sharon knew each other because Doreen's grandparents lived in Lestock, Saskatchewan, where Sharon was born and raised.

When we met in the Willow Inn in Kelowna, Jack and I couldn't get a word in edgewise because Sharon and Doreen had a lot to talk about. This was cool because they liked each other.

We didn't stay in Kelowna as we aimed toward Vancouver, where we had friends. We didn't have jobs to go to but we had a little cash to tide us over.

The city of Vancouver was intimidating but not scary. The challenge was to get a job. We both went on a job search. I ended up working for Wometco. They were distributors for Coca-Cola in the Vancouver area as well as bottling. Sharon applied at Cominco in Vancouver, where she had worked for in Calgary. They hired her in a hurry.

A place to live was next on the list. At this time we lived with Bob and Marg Fontaine, who were originally from Swift Current. They were friends of Brent Gloekler who was a friend of mine also from Swift Current. He was as close to a hippy as I'd ever been friends with. Long hair, into Mary Jane, and owned a monkey. This was an overall swing around from Calgary.

We scored a furnished basement suite from a staunch religious woman. With the help of Sharon's rings she had from her fiancé, we impersonated a newlywed couple, and life went on living in our suite in Vancouver.

This went on until the Teamster's Union moved into Wometco. This meant sign up or quit. I hated unions so this only gave me one option. I quit. The only thing was there was no job to go to except back to Teledyne in Calgary.

Sharon wasn't quitting her job, so I left her in Vancouver with the promise that I would be back in the spring. We weren't engaged so only the promise bonded us.

I left for Calgary by plane and joined Teledyne. We worked nonstop until February in many places across Saskatchewan, Alberta, and British Columbia. We moved a lot so there wasn't much time to get settled in anywhere.

I flew out to Vancouver on a break in February.

This was the part I didn't expect. I picked Sharon up at noon for lunch, and we went to the White Spot restaurant, where she exclaimed in the parking lot, "Are we getting married or what?"

This was not in my plans but I thought, *Why not?* So I said, "Well, I suppose we could try it."

That was the proposal, and we proceeded to make plans.

She gave notice to quit her job, and I went back to Calgary to finish the winter's work.

We did some northern work, and by the end of March, the ice was breaking up, so we were shut down.

I was in the bar waiting for a flight to Vancouver when a man approached our table. He asked if he could sit down. He was heavily bearded and looked like he was some kind of bum. Far from it. His name was Siegfried Boucher from Switzerland. He was a longtime explorer of the Northwest Territories, Yukon, and the Arctic. He was putting together a seismic crew to explore the High Arctic.

The more he talked the drunker I got. He already knew my name. and he had searched me out because I had the shooting license for the Northwest Territories and British Columbia. He wanted me and sweetened the pot to entice me.

I said I would come onboard, but I had to go to Vancouver for four days first because I was engaged to a girl there.

"That's fine," he said, "but be back in four days."

I was back in four days and went to the shop, where all the equipment was being built and loaded into a Hercules air transport plane. Most of the equipment fit into the Herc because the pieces were all under 1,000 lbs in weight.

This was because this time of the year (April) the ice was still only three feet thick on the Arctic Ocean, where we were going. This area was the Ellef Ringnes Island off King Christian Island. This was all very intriguing to me, and I was excited.

When I was on my short four-day trip back to Vancouver to see Sharon, I was full of stories to justify going back to work up north for another two months. I felt guilty enough about leaving Sharon there alone before. I had sweet-talked her into leaving Calgary, quitting a job and career she loved, and ending an engagement with her fiancé. Now I was leaving again for somewhere I wasn't really sure about myself or if I would make it back. There was danger in this venture for sure.

But there was one thing that drew me toward this Arctic venture: money. This was the catalyst, and I knew that if we were getting married in July we would need money, and lots of it.

The promise of good money for a two-month work was enough for me.

As we worked on equipment and loaded the last of the little drilling rigs and tents in wooden boxes on sleigh runners, we were being briefed constantly by Siegfried. He was our coach, leader, boss, and teacher. He had been exploring the Arctic since 1948 mostly by dog sleigh, and he was all-knowing in where we were headed.

This was Siegfried's dream, and everything was now on the line to prove that a small outfit like Phoenix Ventures could outdo the big boys, such as GSI (Geophysical Services Inc.)—who was partly owned by Elvis Presley at that time—Teledyne, and SSC, who were all the big guys in this field.

Our seismic instrumentation to record all the data we were to gather up was Telecommander, from France. This was the newest recorder worth over one million dollars, which in 1972 was a lot of money. These instruments were the key to this operation.

I was only responsible for the shooting (dynamite) part. Along with this responsibility came one other duty: drilling! I had never drilled before, and I wasn't sure what I was getting into. This would come later when we got up to the project.

We left Calgary on an Electra transport plane. The Hercules had already gone before us with most of the equipment. We sat in the Electra with more equipment and supplies and flew 2,200 miles North for seven hours. When we left Calgary, it was minus twenty degrees Fahrenheit. When we arrived at King Christian Island, where the main camp was, it was plus thirty-two degrees Fahrenheit. I remember thinking, *This is great!* The weather in the High Arctic was not much different than Calgary's, warm one day, and cold the next.

Little did I realize that the next morning we woke up in our base camp to minus forty with a fifty-mile-an-hour wind. Lord, it was cold.

We had breakfast at five in the morning and started to assemble the equipment that had to be taken apart to fit into the transport planes. This we did by hand, with fingers bare to the elements. This was when I first regretted coming on this excursion. A walk in the park it was not.

But we got everything together and fired up the passe-partouts (snowmobiles from Quebec). We headed out in a train of little Tonka Toy-type stuff to the amusement of a lot of guys watching from camp.

Guys who were on drilling rigs, driving big machines with big balloon tires and big power. I felt a little embarrassed, but Siegfried laughed at them all. He told us, "You'll see when we're done what we will accomplish!" We could only believe him.

The surveyors had already started flagging the project before we got there. We traveled to the start of the project and set camp. This entailed setting up the kitchen, the sleepers, and the mechanical shop.

The kitchen came in two boxes, which were hinged and opened up. A plastic cover lifted out and formed a tent. These two boxes were like a tent trailer, only on sleigh runners. This was our eating place and our office meeting room. Bathroom that was only by hand washing one person at a time. The average to have a hand bath is about once a week. We were pretty smelly most of the time. Our toilet was of the outside nature.

This was roughing it, but we adjusted. We did what we had to do. I was familiar with the rough nature of living because I had lived this scene back home in Saskatchewan on the farm. For once, I was grateful for my upbringing.

One of the main partners in this project was Dale Payne from Calgary. He was a geophysicist, a surveyor, and a Mormon bishop. This was where the bulk of the crew came from: Calgary and the Mormon church. There were eleven Mormons with us.

They were good people, and they worked hard. Seigfried, the cook (from Westlock, Alberta), the surveyors, my codriller/shooter, and I were the only ones not Mormon.

We started drilling through the ice to load the dynamite one hundred feet into the cold Arctic seawater to get ahead of the recording crew. We started out drilling seven feet of ice and things went well. We made five miles in the first day. Every quarter mile we drilled a hole and placed a charge of dynamite. That was four holes per mile.

Away we went drilling and loading charges, and we worked sixteen hours per day. We didn't have time to get homesick because we were too busy.

As we progressed, we averaged ten miles per day, which was unheard of. We were proud, and we shot over one thousand miles of the Arctic Ocean by the time we finished. We were being paid by the mile in bonuses besides a base pay.

In the six weeks, I made $7,000, which was fantastic, and everything Seigfried had told me that night in the bar in Calgary came to fruition. I was happy in the end.

Our hardships were only a few. The polar bears attacked us twice in the small camp. There was no protection from them. They have no enemies. Loud noise is all that keeps them at bay. If you see them first. We had 303 rifles sent up to us from Calgary. We were instructed to just shoot over the head and not at the bears. If you only wound one they won't stop. This worked, and the noise of the snow machines kept them away. One large male polar bear stalked us for two days and two nights but came no closer than 200 yards. He was waiting for the chance he didn't get—to have us as a meal.

The mechanic shot behind a 400-lb two-year-old cub, and the bullet ricocheted up to wound him. We had to kill that one. That was the only one. A mother bear had twin cubs that she was hiding from the male. She went hunting for food and the father bear found the twins and ate them both. This was interesting, and many years later I found out that this was a bear habit. The male kills the offspring to re-mate with the female. Cruel, but Mother Nature's that way.

The other danger was what we all feared before we went up to the isolated for north. It was the danger of being stranded. We eventually ended up one hundred miles offshore on the Arctic Ocean. This was not flat ice. There are mountains of ice rising up because of the breaking up and re-freezing. This is called second-year and third-year ice. As in the mountains with rocks, this is a similar terrain. Navigating some of this ice can be tricky. We had excellent surveyors, and they flagged our course.

One day, however, we were in the midst of a whiteout. This was where the sky and the land are one. This makes it almost impossible to see where you are going. This one day was the only day we were unable to work.

We didn't know at that time, but when our supply/support plane, a single Otter, touched down to land and bring us supplies, the pilot broke the side of the rudder off, and knowing the pilot was in trouble, lifted off again and went back to King Christian Island to be repaired.

We had no communication except for radios and had no idea the pilot was even in trouble. Consequently, we had no plane for seven days. We were running out of food, fuel, and most importantly, mail. We needed mail to connect us with civilization. We kept working, but we were worried.

The one day that we had to stay in camp was the one day I will never forget.

Music was important to me. This was the luxury we didn't have during this project. Radio was impossible to receive. We were only 700 miles from Siberia. We were north of the magnetic north pole, and things like radios were unheard of.

The surveyor, younger than me, was a great guy. He was from Switzerland, spoke good English, and had an eight-track tape player. We visited my tent that day listening to Bob Dylan, and he just happened to have some weed. This was taboo, but he shared and we mellowed out for the day. We knew the danger we were in, but somehow, this day was like a dream.

I lay back and thought of all the situations I had been in before when I should have been killed and thought, *Is this how my life will end up here in the land of no people?*

I thought back to when I shared a log cabin kitchenette with another shooter in Calgary on Macleod Trail. His name was Gabby (John) Goleski, and we were both working for Teledyne. We shared a pickup of Teledyne's to get back and forth because his car broke down and my Firebird was in the body shop.

He had to go to the dentist one day and used the truck. I took a cab to the motel and made supper. He came in drunk with two bottles of wine. I had one small glass, as I wasn't into partying at this period because I was very broke and I was afraid to drink with him anyway.

The more he drank the worse he got. He was loud, belligerent, and a pure asshole.

He went to the bathroom, came out, and said, "Where are the keys to the truck? I'm going to see my aunt."

I said, "I don't know, Gabby. You were driving it."

He went into the bedroom, and I was on the couch watching TV. I thought he was done for the night. No such luck. He came out with a bullet vest full of shotgun shells and a twelve-gauge shotgun in his hand.

He said, "Give me the keys, McGregor, you son of a bitch."

I was shocked and jumped up not thinking, but I'm sure I grabbed the gun barrel. We wrestled with the gun between us, and I reached for the phone on the wall that connected us to the desk, where they put the phone calls through and connected the room by giving them the number we wanted.

I got the person on the phone looking after the office, who was also the manager of the motel. Gabby overpowered me, and I ran for the door of the motel room. Luckily, it opened and I escaped. There were four shots, and I was scared out of my mind. I was unhurt and appeared at the office desk, much to the amazement of the manager. I was white as a ghost, I guess. and alive. The Calgary Police Canine Service brought a dog and arrested Gabby.

I was asked to press charges for attempted murder, but I wouldn't do that for fear of reprisal. He was taken to Ponoka for thirty days of observation and was rehired by Teledyne as a shooter again.

We met up again in Peace River, where he was going to do it all over again because he blamed me for what happened. And as for his missing clothes, I knew nothing about that, and he wouldn't believe me. He was drunk again, and I held it against Teledyne for sending him to Peace River, where I was running a crew. Work and money were Teledyne's priority, and human resources was not.

I thought about this while we were stoned this day and lying in this little tent in a box in the High Arctic.

I thought that night in Calgary would have been a more dramatic way to die. This was only one of the near-death experiences I had had in the previous twenty-five years of my life: the car accidents, the guy who used to look after the swimming pool in Gull Lake holding me by gunpoint for three hours and threatening to kill me, and the close times of suicide when I was feeling so sorry for myself after days and weeks of drinking and bad love affairs. All of these situations seemed so much more likely to have ended my days than freezing and starving to death, I thought.

After the traumatic seven days without air support, the whiteout, and the fear that we may succumb to the elements, we forged ahead with the project sat out before us as no other crew had ever accomplished. We were all very proud of ourselves, and we were congratulated many times by our superiors. Our crew, with its many different personalities, religions, and nationalities, gelled together like a sports team would, and our chemistry, although at times abrasive, was such that we bonded to achieve more than we thought we could. We were written into a story in Oil Week Magazine that summer, and we felt good about it. The next winter, Siegfried and Dale Payne tried to repeat this venture, but I didn't go, and a lot of the crew didn't go back. The accomplishment we had was not to be repeated ever again.

We returned to Calgary from King Christian Island in late May 1972. We had no summer clothes with us, and upon arrival at Calgary Industrial Airport, we were attired in our winter parkas and heavy insulated underwear. When we boarded the Electra aircraft in King Christian Island, it was twenty degrees below zero. When we arrived in Calgary, it was seventy degrees above zero. We were very hot, embarrassed, and anxious to get a room to change our clothes. So consequently I had to go shopping for clothes. That was a hilarious episode for the clerk at the Hudson Bay store.

I felt like a trapper coming into the city after six months in the bush. I got changed and booked a flight to Vancouver, where Sharon was waiting patiently.

Vancouver was warm, flowery, and beautiful even in its smog and smell of diesel, factory farms, and noise. The contrast between the quiet mess, cleanliness, and freshness of the far North was incredible. The two lifestyles were an adjustment not only physically but mentally as well. This is why even today I love the North away from the cities. The North is still virtually untouched by man and is a land that God intended for man to inhabit when he created the earth.

# CHAPTER 19

## The Wedding

Sharon, my bride to be, had been busy planning our wedding. This was a big deal for her family too. They were Hungarian and Slavic. I had yet to meet her family, and I wasn't sure what was ahead.

Sharon had traded her Vauxhall Viva car off for a 1970 Dodge Coronet two-door hardtop with a 318 V8. It was a nice car, but I would have preferred a Malibu Chev. Nonetheless, the car was great, and we were ready to head back to Saskatchewan to meet Mom and Dad and the rest of the family. Sharon had another week to finish at Cominco to fulfill her commitment of two weeks' notice, because she wanted to reapply after we were married to go back to Calgary to work for them again. They treated Sharon like gold in Vancouver, and we were happy for that.

After the long winter's work up North, I had quite a wad of cash. I was prepared to pay my share of the wedding because I had no support from my family to chip in, as usually was the custom.

That was fine with me. I preferred to pay my own way if I could.

This was not to be, however. Sharon's dad, Bill, would have none of that. He paid all the expenses for the wedding. No arguing could change his mind. He was as stubborn as I was, and this stubbornness would come into play many times in the future.

While I was waiting for Sharon to finish her work commitment, my friend Brent Gloekler and I hung out. We slowly loaded Sharon and my belongings into the Coronet to pack for the trip to Saskatchewan.

While we killing time in Vancouver we decided to go to Blaine, Washington, to play golf one day. We crossed into the States from Canada through the Peace

Arch. This was easy, no problems. We golfed the day away and headed back to Canada. It was not so easy though, as we were asked what all the stuff was in the car and we couldn't explain well enough. We had to unload and spread everything out to make sure there was no contraband. Brent had long hair and a ponytail, and I always blamed him for the cause of our problem that day.

Sharon finished her job, and we said our goodbyes to Bob and Marg Fontaine, my buddy Brent, and several other good friends.

The one that we felt bad about saying goodbye to was our land lady, who was so motherly to Sharon while I was away for so long and who turned out to be the kindest woman you could imagine. Especially when we first met her, she was so staunch and strict, which prompted us to pretend we were married to fool her into renting us the furnished basement suite. I'm sure she was never fooled.

Vancouver was a beginning for us, a trial period, and a testing of our love for each other. This short period of time to live together out of wedlock was accepted by most people but still frowned on by many.

This was also the longest period of time I had ever been true to one girl. I always bragged at that time that I wasn't in love with Sharon, and I would bet that the relationship would never last more than six months if we got married.

How wrong I was, as the future would prove. Time creates more love, and we had lots of time to create.

We left Vancouver with no regrets and no debts, and the windshield of the Dodge Coronet was our looking glass to the future.

Through the Roger's Pass, past Banff and Lake Louise and stopping only in Calgary, we headed for Lestock, Saskatchewan. In anticipation of the welcoming are arms of a family mixed with Hungarian and Slavic and love for anyone who was loved by one of their own.

I needed to be loved by them. I also needed to prove that I was worthy of their acceptance. This I overdid by telling stories that glorified my past in the seismic/oil and gas exploration adventures I had been through.

They were mesmerized by these tales, and I was somebody totally different from their way of life.

We arrived at Lestock, where there are seven Indian reserves. There were natives all over the highway on the way between Raymore and Lestock. I wondered about this, but I had lots of experience in the North with natives so I wasn't too worried. The common thread of these people is poverty. As in any native community, Lestock hotel was the focal point for them and the white people always owned these establishments.

This is a problem much too complex to get into by me. Historians can't even figure this out.

Sharon's family lived three miles north of Lestock. There were two ways to get there: one was on a dirt road traveled in good weather; the other was two miles further but on good gravel. We chose the short route and pulled up the long driveway. A gate was across the driveway, and I hated it. But it was a necessary gate to keep the cattle from the road. I always tried to talk Sharon's dad into putting in a Texas gate, and I even hauled one from Alberta, but it never got installed. I think he was afraid a cow or calf would get hung up, and he was an animal lover of the best kind. He hated to see an animal suffer.

I got out, opened the gate, and drove into the yard, showing the family watching from the house that I was a gentleman.

I was wearing shorts, and that in itself would be a sight. I had good legs, but they weren't meant to be exposed. I didn't care how I looked at that stage of my life. I was more concerned about who I was about to meet because I was marrying into their family.

Bill was the head of the family; there was no doubt about that. He was small in stature but big in life. He was the focal point, full of life, and he would always take charge of any situation. He didn't do this by fear or control of others but by being sincere and by questioning you to get you to open up to him and feeling special.

This was the impression I got from him, and he stuck out his strong calloused hand welcoming me to the family.

Sharon's mother, Jean, was standing behind Bill, but she was very much in control of all that was happening in the family. She was smart and perceptive, and I knew I would like her. I'm happy she accepted me because I would have hated to have her reject me.

For some reason she liked me enough to always defend me. For this, I would be grateful later on.

Next was Anne, Sharon's grandmother, who was a widow because Sharon's grandfather had passed on years before.

Granny was independent, and she was all-knowing in the ways of survival. She had gone through hard times and knew a lot about how to get by with nothing. She was a kind and gentle woman that everyone loved and respected. I admired her for her deep, quiet intelligence.

Next were the siblings. Sharon was the oldest, so the next was her brother Gerry, who was long on ambition, very smart in school, and had big dreams.

Keith was the youngest boy and was full of energy. He loved life and fun. Not to confuse fun with responsibility, however. He was always conscientious, but sometimes he would be led in the wrong direction by friends who weren't so respectable.

Keith looked up to me from the beginning. I was leading the kind of life that appealed to him. I loved that kid, and we hunted gophers, played the guitar, and drank together even though he was much younger. We were very close from the start.

The third sibling was Debbie. She was only ten years old, but you could tell that she was very smart, cunning, and manipulative. She was a very pretty girl with a dark complexion. She would in the future make me proud, and then we would lock horns for many years, which I would consider lost years between us.

At this point, nothing mattered except the upcoming wedding.

I met the Beres family that hot day in June 1972. It was a day that would change my life more than I could ever imagine at that time. It was a turning point from irresponsible freedom to make my own mistakes, of which there were many in the previous twenty-six years.

I was totally insecure in the fact that I wasn't going to fit in with the stable family, who worked very hard for all they had and appreciated life more than material things. The Catholic religion was also important to the Beres family. I was a Protestant and far from practicing, but my early years were still important to me when I was totally involved with the United Church.

I still had a grudge from my sister Lois's turning Catholic and all the anger expressed over that by my dad Hector, as I explained earlier.

I was unsure about marrying into a Catholic family, but I wasn't about to convert, so that was justified in my mind and seemed to be fine with Hector.

By this time Hector was seventy years old, had long given up on life, and was only concerned with where the next bottle of whiskey was coming from. However, his approval was still important to me.

This proved how insecure I was. I was getting married without a job, a home, and with minimal money. I'm still not sure why Sharon, my bride-to-be, wanted to forge ahead into a life of insecurity with me.

I wondered why she gave up her engagement to her previous fiancé from Lestock. He was from a stable, well-to-do family and had good looks, education, and a rosy future.

This was a big decision for me. I wasn't quite ready to get married, but I recognized the opportunity for some stability in my life, which I had never had up to this point.

The partying, the alcohol, the times in jail, the depressions, the don't-give-a-shit attitude, the women of my past—of which there were many—all of these things would have to change. This is what marriage meant to me.

I remember when I was between seismic projects and living with my sister Vangie in Calgary in 1967. This was also a turning point in my life that didn't turn out the way it was supposed to.

I was twenty-one years old, had a nice car, money, and girls, girls, and girls. I indulged in all that were available to me and drank myself to the point of depression, where I fell very fast and hard. I was as close to suicide as a person could get.

For some reason I called Alcoholics Anonymous. It was Sunday and two wonderful AA members came to Forest Lawn, where my sister lived. My brother-in-law Rudy was in Egypt at that time working on an electrical contract for Pan American Oil.

I was agitated, depressed, and a total mess. I had no one to turn to who could understand.

The two AA guys took me to downtown Calgary to the Alano Club, where recovering alcoholics met to support each other and try to live by the Big Book of A.A.

They saved my life at that point. This was the only other major turning point I could say was for the best. This was what I thought about while I was deciding whether I should get married or not.

I spent only three months in AA at that point, but those three months would prove to be something I could fall back on and draw solace from as years went on.

I hung out at the farm of Sharon's dad for two weeks, but I made a deal with Sharon that I'll leave her there to plan the wedding and I would take a trip to Gull Lake, Swift Current, and Calgary to say goodbye to the single life.

Why she agreed to this plan of mine I will never know, but she did, and I went off to assure myself that I was doing the right thing by getting married.

I left Lestock and renewed with old acquaintances, drank with old buddies, met up with some old girl friends, and finally wound up at Mom and Dad's place in Gull Lake.

At this time, they were living in an old shack in town. They had sold their farm to my sister Lois and her husband, Jim Piechotta. This was a bad event in the way it happened, and my dad had a grudge against our family for having to sell the farm, but he wouldn't admit he only lost everything he worked for with his drinking.

They were totally broke and living on the old-age pension and welfare money. Booze was king, and I felt so sorry for them, but there was little I could do. Dad was stubborn and proud. There was no reasoning with him. I had a small knowledge of AA, and I knew he was one who could benefit from it but was of little help then because I was drinking again at this point.

You can't tell someone they have a problem when you have the same problem and you don't set an example.

I was wishing on a star. But I needed reassurance from Mom and Dad that I was okay to get married. I didn't get this from them. They weren't too concerned about my future, and this time with them was more of a depression period for me.

There was one thing I came away with from this five-day soul-searching: the determination and promise I made to myself that I would never end up in the state they ended up in. This time spent away from Sharon made my mind up to take the opportunity that was in front of me. I went back to Lestock thinking that I wanted what the Beres family had: stability, security, and a better life than what I had in the past.

I was putting the past behind me, and I was excited to enter the future.

# CHAPTER 20

## The Wedding—Hungarian Style

July 8 was the date set for our wedding—a Saturday, with the odds in favor of a good weather.

The stag party was set up for me at the Beres farm. This was uncomfortable at first because I didn't know anybody other than Bill, Keith, and Gerry.

However, everyone I did meet welcomed me as one of their own, and I made one friend, who still remains so, in Sharon's neighbor, Teddy Vass. He is a true Hungarian and a funny kind of guy, who made me laugh and have fun at an otherwise boring party. Eating was the name of the game at any gathering put on by these farm people, who struggled to carve an existence farming on land that was at the best times unkind.

Food to me at a party was spoiling a hundred-dollar drunk on a two-dollar meal. I very seldom ate when I drank. This was better for me, and Sharon's mother recognized this in me. She made sure I had plenty to eat when I was drinking.

The stag party they put on for me helped introduce me to the community, but I couldn't help wondering if my friends from Gull Lake and Calgary were closer and what would have happened if they had been there. I'm sure there would have been more colorful stories to tell.

Last-minute details were attended to, and the church was waiting for the happening.

I had to meet the priest of the Lestock Catholic Church. At this meeting, we discussed my marriage to one of their parishioners, Sharon, who was faithfully brought up as a Catholic.

This was funny in the sense that both Sharon and I were not churchgoers, and we had been living in sin in the eyes of the church. This was hypocrisy at its best.

We put on a veil of secrecy and proceeded with the ways of the church.

One thing I didn't like was signing the rights to religious upbringing of any future children from Sharon and me to the Catholic Church.

I had very little choice. I was either to go with the plan or ruin all the plans this wonderful bunch of friends and relatives had planned for Sharon and me.

My religious convictions weren't strong enough to circumvent the Catholic way of life, so "let the plans proceed" was my decision.

This decision never interfered with our lives. My religion stayed the same and was supported by AA in the future. The Catholic influence was only through the baptisms of our three children.

This was a much better solution than me turning Catholic like my poor sister Lois did when she married the Polish Catholic many years before. This is unacceptable to millions of Protestants and causes many problems people don't need when you are starting a marriage.

The priest was kind and understanding a rancher himself part time. He was also a hardworking man. I liked him so I respected his views. He was a good priest for us to have performed our ceremony.

I drove to Gull Lake to pick up my dad and mom to bring them back to Lestock.

They hadn't met anyone from Sharon's family, and we thought they could get to know the Beres family prior to the wedding.

Mom and Dad stayed with Sharon's granny in Lestock because things were way too busy at the farm getting things ready for the reception after the wedding. This was the big deal, and no one had time to babysit my mom and dad. *Babysitting* was the appropriate word because both mom and dad at that time were alcoholics. Booze was number one for them, and it was not only sad but also embarrassing for Sharon and me.

Granny was excellent with them and had all kinds of tricks to limit their drinking.

I'm sure Mom and Dad were uncomfortable too. Alcoholics aren't stupid people, just sick of a disease that makes them wallow in self-pity. Living in the past is the flavor of the day for alcoholics.

My mom and dad could play this game of reminiscing better than anyone I ever knew.

I called this "digging up bones." I learned the game well myself and played this game many times. I tried to spend as much time as I could with them, but I fell short because I would get frustrated and pissed off.

One thing I was happy about was the wedding date. July 8 was also my dad's birthday. He turned seventy on July 8, 1972.

I thought this was cool, so did everyone else except Hector.

He passed this off as just another year older for him. He hated getting older. He blamed age for his downfall, and I inherited this attribute from him later in life.

The week passed as all weeks do, and the wedding day dawned with rain. "Oh shit," we all said in unison.

I looked at the weather and thought, *Cloud, rain, and no sunshine, the story of my life. Let's party.* These types of days were always party days in Seismic.

We couldn't work when it rained in Seismograph because the rain affected the geophones. We called the clouds on those days of rainouts as Beer Clouds.

So this was fine by me, to have rain on our wedding day. Some of our best parties were in the mud, blood, and spilled beer and whiskey.

Sharon had stayed the night before the wedding at her granny's house. I was at the farm.

I got dressed in my suit, had a couple of whiskies, and got in the car with Gerry and Keith, Sharon's brothers. Off we went to the church to get me married.

I'll always remember the song that came on while we were driving the three miles to town. "Long Cool Woman in the Black Dress" by the Hollies was the last song of my single life.

As was the case when I lost my virginity, the turning point in my life was marked by an appropriate song to be instilled in my memory forever.

When the song was over, we were in front of the huge church in Lestock.

Everyone was seated, and I was escorted to a private room to wait for further instructions.

My best man of course was Jack O'Connor. This was important to me. Jack was happy to oblige. He figured that I would be better off married because he had already married Sharon's friend Doreen from the same area.

The bridal party was made up of the following: Diane Trywitt, the maid of honor and Sharon's friend; Doreen O'Connor, the bridesmaid and Sharon's friend; Debbie Beres, the junior bridesmaid and Sharon's sister; Jack O'Connor, the best man and my best friend; Gerry Beres, the second best man and Sharon's brother; and Keith Beres, the third best man and Sharon's little brother.

Standing at the altar with my best men, we watched as Sharon was escorted by her proud father, Bill. Bill was a character, and he was well respected in the community of Lestock. Bill was small in stature but big in voice and actions that he stood out in a crowd even at five foot six. He spoke both Hungarian and English very well and knew some Ukrainian and Cree. Bill got along very well with everyone he met in life.

Watching Sharon and Bill made me wonder if I could ever take the number one place in her life that she had always reserved for her dad.

They looked great coming down the aisle, and the full white wedding gown was a fantastic sight.

I was proud and nervous. When I get nervous, I try to make jokes, but I found nothing funny to come up with. I just kept quiet and hope I wasn't going to screw up the ritual.

The vows were taken. The priest wore cowboy boots that were sticking out from under his white ceremonial robe. Sharon and I signed the register of marriage on that summer day of July 8, 1972. The prayers were said, the songs were sung, and our names were entered into the book of marriage in the Catholic Church in Lestock, Saskatchewan.

The hard part was over, and we walked together through the doors of the church that opened onto a beautiful sunshine-filled day. The sun came out while we were being married, and the rain and clouds had disappeared.

This in itself was a miracle to the old people at the church. Many people in attendance that day were superstitious, and this they said was a very good sign.

They tell us many times that day that we would be blessed with a long marriage. It seems they were right.

I could only think as we were exiting the church, *Now what?* I knew I had to provide a future or I'd look pretty dumb to everyone watching that day. Success was foremost in my mind that day, but I had no idea what was ahead.

God, I wished I had a plan, but, oh well, let's party hard and let tomorrow wait.

The crowd migrated to the community hall down the street. We went for picture-taking, as all weddings must.

My favorite part was bombing around Lestock with our Dodge Coronet decorated and sporting the Alberta license plate.

I was the Alberta stranger to anyone who was watching that day, and I was proud of it.

So there I was, married, almost broke, and no job. Life was good.

My family was there that day: Lois, Malcolm, Orville, Doreen, and Vangie.

I was the last to get married, and this was important to them. I was glad my family was there. It was proof to the Beres family that we had some substance even though we were a little dysfunctional.

Our family knew how to party and have fun. We knew how to handle any occasion and fit in well with the Hungarian crowd of people that day.

The reception was fantastic, of course. You knew that Jean, Sharon's mother, and her friends would not have anything less than perfect.

Sharon was the firstborn and the first to be married so this was a big deal for Jean. Jean was all over the place like a hawk, everything was done right on time, and the reception was perfect.

The speeches, the toasts, and the congratulations all were as should be, and my speech was well-rehearsed in English and part-Hungarian. This was drummed into me for many days and I said my piece of Hungarian, which meant, "thank you very much and have a good time."

The crowd loved and appreciated the effort to recognize the people I was marrying into.

There is no race of people I don't try to understand if I become intertwined with them. I appreciate the differences, and I've gotten along well with all nationalities and colors by expressing an interest. There are good and bad, but anyone can sort out the bad ones. The good ones are like cream in milk and always rise to the top. These are the people I learn from, and I always have had a knack of gaining acceptance in a crowd.

There was a presentation where the wedding party stands behind a long row of tables and the crowd files by offering their congratulations by having a drink with the groom and a hug and kiss with the bride. I thought it would be rude to not drink with anyone so I had a shot-for-shot with all who wanted to. Needless to say, I got very drunk by the time we were finished. I was still standing and walked out to escape to our car waiting to rumble to Fort Qu'Appelle, where we had a bridal suite booked for the wedding night.

Sharon drove and I passed out. I still don't remember the night, but it was short.

We traveled back to Lestock the next morning for gift-opening and started the party all over. My family was in full swing and had partied all night. They were making the most of the weekend and weren't wasting their time sleeping.

Inevitably in our family, drinking leads to arguing, and arguing is a forerunner to fighting. This wedding was no exception.

The fights between Lois and whoever pisses her off were legendary. She never was a fan of too much drinking and impressed this on many drinkers who crossed her path.

My sister Doreen had gone through a divorce at this period and hooked up with a guy named Chester, a rig push who drank way too much. Lois and Chester locked horns, and the fight was on. Welcome to the McGregor family, Chester. He lost the fight but never forgave Lois afterward.

I laughed because I knew he was in for a knockout punch. Other than that incident, everything was fine the first day after our wedding. The gifts were opened, the donations were counted, and the mess was cleaned up.

Normality and reality were next, and they were to happen on Monday.

# CHAPTER 21

---

# Alberta-Bound Again
# (with a bride)

The emotional letdown after the wedding, planning, worrying, and the actual event was finally much like a depression. We hung out at the farm for a few days vegging out and I was getting way to comfortable and spoiled by Sharon's mom. I thought maybe I should have married her instead.

We rented a U-haul trailer and loaded up all the gifts we had received and headed to the bright lights of Calgary, Alberta. We had received cash to the amount of $1,500 from everyone at the presentation and cash gifts, plus Sharon's mom and dad slipped in a little extra.

From that point on, I let Sharon take care of the money because I was terrible with cash. There was a hole in every pocket, and cash just seemed to slip through.

This was a good decision because later on she would handle all the financial end of our affairs, which would become a much bigger responsibility than we could imagine at this point in our lives.

We arrived in Calgary and looked for a place to live. An apartment was available off Macleod Trail in a high rise. We liked it, and I bought enough furniture to make it livable to the point where we could watch TV, listen to music, cook, eat, and sleep. What more do two people just married need? Life was good. Life was simple, and life was happy.

Sharon went back to the old job she had quit at Cominco, which was close by.

I had no job. This to some guys would have been enough, but to me, having no job was awful. I was bored and edgy. I had to do something. I had made a deal with Sharon that I wouldn't work in Seismic again, but there wasn't much available at this time.

An advertisement popped up in the want ads for a shooter within the Northwest Territories with a dynamite license and experience with Industrial First Aid.

Here's where I went back on my word to Sharon. I sweet-talked her into letting me apply.

She agreed, and I applied to London, England. I was interviewed and hired, but there was a waiting period until the Hovercraft from London arrived at Shingle Point, Northwest Territories by barge.

It was two weeks before I was flown to Yellowknife then by floatplane to a small lake close to camp at Shingle Point. Shingle Point is one of the locations for the DEW line. There was one of the huge white domes for radar that you see. DEW stands for "distant early warning," and these radar stations were set up to defend against invasion from foreign countries mainly by the USA. The Alaska Highway was also part of this defense system.

The Easter egg stood out in the barren landscape of tundra and was built on the shore of the Beaufort Sea.

The Beaufort Sea was our objective and the offshore project we were exploring. Imperial Oil was the client, and Seismic Services Inc. had been contracted to shoot the shallow waters to determine the feasibility of drilling.

The key to this venture was the hovercraft. It had a jet engine and airlift system that would raise the structure off the water and propel ahead skimming the water at speeds up to eighty miles per hour.

This was an eye-opening sight for me. I had never even seen pictures of anything like this before.

SSI had purchased this hovercraft from the Israeli Army after the Israel-Egypt six-day war was over. They had used this as a gunship in the desert. It was capable of land and sea travel. The Israelis removed the guns, and SSI took it to London, where they equipped it with Seismic instruments for Seismic surveys. They loaded it into a ship and transported it to Canada. They then offloaded it and sent it by barge down the St. Lawrence Seaway. From there, they loaded it on to a train and choochooed it to Hay River. From there they barged it to the Beaufort Sea.

This was a long trip for what turned out to be a short job. This must have all been worthwhile because the drilling started after our job was finished.

To me it seemed like a lot of expense and work, but I was naïve to the economics at that stage of my life.

The crew was made up of Englishmen, and everyone had been part of the army. They had all served two years and had all been in Ireland fighting the IRA.

The hovercraft required a pilot and navigator because it was an airborne machine.

My two helpers were much more experienced with explosives than me, but they had to work under my license of the Northwest Territories. They weren't too happy, but I didn't play boss so we got along fine. These two men were very rough, tough, and would snap at any time. They were fantastic workers, and they didn't fool around.

The job we had was dangerous because we stood on the back of the hovercraft reeling out three strands of Primacord explosives of one hundred feet in length. This is a plastic rope, and an electrical cap is attached to the end. The Primacord is let out into the water then the hovercraft lets out the air from the huge bags it sits on. The motor is cut and we would shoot the 300 feet of explosives to create sound waves that would refract off the geological formations below the water. The sound waves would then be recorded and translated to see if there was an indication of oil and gas. This is a simple explanation of what we did.

They sent divers from Ottawa to dive and record how many fish we were killing on each shot. We allowed only thirty-five on each shot and passed the test, so we were allowed to carry on.

I often wondered if we had killed over thirty-five fish if they would have abandoned the program. That would have been a lot of expense for nothing.

The Beluga whales were at the end of their spawning period at that time, and we had to wait until they finished before we could even start.

This was in 1972, and even then the environment was important. *This was a good thing*, I thought.

We also had Eskimos working with us. The names all started with Eskimo—Eskimo George, Eskimo Ed, and Eskimo Dan—and they were awesome people. They were happy, helpful, and all-knowing on land and sea.

We shot all of August and September until the ice started to form. The project was over, and the hovercraft was loaded for its long trek back to Australia.

They were headed to Australia from Shingle Point, and I was asked if I wanted to go. I flatly refused; that would have ended my short marriage, which I hadn't had much time to enjoy. "No," I said. I was going back to Calgary. "I've had enough of you Limies." They all laughed and made many jokes about Canadians.

We were float planed into Inuvik, where we all had rooms booked for the night until the plane left for Calgary.

We headed for the Zoo, which was the Inuvik Inn Bar. We proceeded to get very drunk, and believe me, the English boys that I worked with could drink, fight, and tell jokes. We had a great time, and I'll never forget those guys. I learned a lot from them, and their knowledge saved my life a few times while we were out on the sea performing this dangerous task.

No one got hurt, and our venture was a huge success resulting in Imperial Oil building offshore islands to drill on.

# CHAPTER 22

## Giving up One Life for Another

Upon arriving back in Calgary, which in itself was like heaven to me, the land of the midnight sun must have lost its glow for me. I was fed up with the long periods away. Now that I had something to come home to, I cared less about the excitement of the northern frontier, and I knew I was missing out on what was supposed to be a partnership between Sharon and me. I had signed the marriage license, so I always considered this a partnership. Later on we would extend this into a business, but for now, I knew I had to quit the long periods away or our marriage wouldn't last.

Sharon was happy working at Cominco. They were a great bunch of people, and we were good friends with her coworkers, namely, Duane, Gordon and Dorothy, Emily, and Judy. These were people of that time whom we partied with, visited their homes, and wanted to have lives like them. My life was not ordinary. I was different in that circle of friends of Sharon's.

After coming back from Shingle Point, I had lots of stories to tell these office workers from Cominco, and they loved the tales of the North.

I was empty inside and I felt inferior because of the fact that I wasn't stable in a job or a career.

I would drink too much and feel sorry that all I had was the experience to do really well in Seismic only. I had to decide: Seismic or a marriage breakup. I knew so many guys in the Seismograph industry who paid alimony and child support because their marriages couldn't stand the strain.

I had jobs during spring breakup and short-lived jobs in British Columbia, but I hated them all. Seismic was what I loved. It was an addiction of a job where I could get away and think outside the box for a few months at a time.

The biggest addiction was when the projects finished as they always did. The off time was fantastic because we would have lots of money, and this would be *party time*. This was the hardest thing to let go of.

At twenty-six years of age, I was mature enough to know I was over with this life. I looked through the want ads in the Albertan paper and Calgary Herald every day. I couldn't find anything that appealed to me.

One day I spotted an ad for a pressure truck driver. "Experience preferred but will train," it said. The ad was from the Bob Miller Oil Services out of Airdrie.

I phoned and talked to a guy named Jim Pagan. Little did I know this phone call was about to change my life forever.

I made the call and set up a time that afternoon to meet with Jim Pagan in Airdrie.

I pulled up to a skid shack that had been set up as an office. There were dozens of trucks of all kinds. This to me looked like a wrecking yard, but I didn't know what the nature of this business was, anyway.

I did know that I needed a job, and I was game to try something different.

Jim Pagan was easy to like. He made me feel welcomed, and the interview was like a visit instead of a grilling. He was also an ex-doodle bugger, which was the nickname for a Seismograph worker. He had been everywhere, just like I had, and we shared some of our experiences.

He hired me that day and I was to start training the next day. Right on! I was excited to tell Sharon when she got home from work. She was happy too and relieved because she was afraid if I sat to long I would go back to Seismic again.

The next day I went to Okotoks where Miller had an old Dodge three ton Pressure truck spotted to pump water down a dispersal well from a four hundred barrel tank spotted to hold water hauled from Quick Creek Gas Plant by Imperial Oil.

One of Bob Miller's men was a sixty-five-year-old man by the name of Bill Price. He had high energy, was on the move constantly, and knew everything about pressure trucks and pressure work.

He taught me enough to get started and left me alone with this truck-pumping water.

For two weeks, I babysat this operation and became very bored. It ran twelve to fourteen hours per day, and I had only the truck drivers coming in every hour or two to break the monotony. I did meet some of the Miller hands during this time. This was sour water, which has H2S or hydrogen sulfide gas in the water. This can be deadly in high concentrations, and I wasn't familiar with the danger yet. I found out much more later about this deadly gas.

Jim Pagan knew that I wouldn't stay there at this same pumping job for too long. He brought me to Airdrie and put me with Bill Price to go along and see what they did at Amoco Crossfield. This gas field was just between Airdrie and Crossfield.

We worked together, and Bill Price was happy with me.

He trained me, and I was fortunate to have learned from someone who had so much experience and dedication to his work. He was fantastic and could work circles around me.

For his age, he was unbelievable.

There was a problem, however. There was a chemical that only Amoco used to dissolve sulfur from the gas well tubing. The tubing is the pipe that is put into the well casing that produces the natural gas from deep underground. The sulfur contains the H2S gas and is yellow in color. The chemical used to dissolve this and keep the gas flowing is called Murox.

Now if you know how obnoxious a skunk smells then multiply that by one hundred to imagine the smell of Murox. This product is also used to odorize propane in small amounts.

If you spilled a drop on your shoes or clothes, this smell would linger forever until you burned or buried your shoes or clothing.

I couldn't handle this odor; I would go back to our apartment in Calgary and leave my boots in the hallway.

One day they brought in a gas detector to see if there was a leak in the building. This was funny, but I couldn't take it anymore.

I went to Jim Pagan and said I would have to quit after only three weeks. He said that I wouldn't be pumping this all the time and that this was unusual that we were pumping so much at one time. He talked me into staying, and I did.

I got into more diversified jobs and got interested in the big picture. I learned more each day and soon, I was on my own.

Being on my own was important to me. I definitely made mistakes starting out, but Jim was an experienced boss and taught me all the ins and outs about pressure pumping.

The trucks I ran weren't fancy, new, or even comfortable. But the one thing that Miller had over his competition was work. He was a master at finding work for us. He was a fantastic salesman and knew everyone in Alberta involved in the oil patch. He had a fantastic memory and a great personality. Bob Miller had another quality. He was shrewd. He could find equipment and trucks that are cheap and make them work as well as any new expensive truck. He would buy wrecked trucks and rebuild them or use them for parts. He never forgot where a part was located if you should need such a part to fix your particular truck.

Careful with his money, Bob Miller survived the poor times of the ever-changing oil patch. He handled the ups and downs very well, and he never laid anyone off if times were slow. He was a master at making a profit.

Bob Miller was the owner, the boss, and the buck stopped with him.

Jim Pagan was a partner in the part of the business called Bob Miller Oil Services Ltd. The main part was Bob Miller Trucking Ltd., which consisted of tank trucks.

The oil service side was run by Jim Pagan, who owned 40 percent. Jim was very knowledgeable in this part and coordinated the work, purchased, and designed the equipment needed for this operation. Jim was my mentor, my boss, and he became my friend.

For two years, I worked diligently running pressure trucks and mobile compressors, and I learned a great deal about high-pressure gas wells and sour oil wells around Alberta.

I was fortunate in the fact that I was trusted to make a lot of decisions on my own and learned to repair, change, and redesign equipment to help make things easier and better in my job.

I was happy and proud of what I did.

One day I walked into the office to have coffee with Jim and Bob. Jim said, "I want you to run the hot oiler."

I said, "No chance."

Jim said, "Well, we lost our operator, Jerry Bjorsvick."

Jerry had taken the Hot Oiler to Olds, Alta, and was running out of Olds, where he lived. He decided that he wanted to move on to battery operating, so he quit working for Miller and left the Hot Oiler operation.

The Hot Oiler was Jim Pagan's pet. This was what he knew best because he had run it for many years. The Hot Oiler was a unique piece of equipment in those days. There were very few around, and people to run them were few and far between.

The concept was like a giant barbeque, fire to heat oil and water prior to being pumped down wells and pipelines. Heating big tanks was another purpose for a Hot Oiler.

Fire plus flammable fluids plus high pressure were three things that made a recipe for disaster.

This was what I thought of a Hot Oiler. I was scared of the contraption.

This unit was on a Chev truck with a screaming six-cylinder diesel motor. A propane fired burner, a 10,000 PSI quintuplex pressure pump and a two-compartment tank. Something else it had are two transmissions; a five-by-four, they called it. I had never driven one of these trucks, and I didn't want to.

Jim talked and I listened, but I wasn't swayed easily. Finally, I said I would try it.

Jim personally trained and showed me a lot of things about hot oiling and how to do things safely.

I related this job to when I was shooting and handling dynamite, and both jobs were dangerous. I had great respect for fire, however, and I started out on this job with respect and fear.

I learned fast, and I covered a lot of Alberta with this truck. I got to know many people because of the different areas I worked in. There weren't too many of these Hot Oilers, so the demand was spread out.

This truck was slow on the road and would only go 50 mph. It was underpowered, and although it had twenty gears with the five-by-four, the power was lacking to move the heavy unit. I hated this; I liked to drive as fast as I could, especially on the #2 highway.

The propane burner was also too small. The delivery of one million BTU per hour was painstakingly slow when heating a 400-barrel tank of water. These faults I found out early, but I was hired to do a job, so I did what I could.

I earned respect because I learned to have confidence in hot-oiling even with an outdated Hot Oiler. Things were changing fast, and there were bigger and better units being built.

I was sent to Turner Valley one very cold day. It was minus forty degrees Fahrenheit.

I arrived on the lease, rigged up, and as we always did, pressure-tested my pump line. While I was testing my line, I was firing up the propane burner to start hot-oiling. The propane froze and came out of the nozzle in lumps of liquid propane. This propane of course didn't light, but the propane turned to vapor. I was lighting the burner with a rag on a wire. The igniter had long ago ceased to function, so the rag/wire trick was the igniter.

When the fire lit, there was a terrific explosion, blowing the top off the heater. I was blown backward to the ground. Of course, the clutch that was in my hand was let go. The pressure pump kept running, and the gauge that was marked to 10,000 PSI wrapped past that, and I was lying half-conscious on my back.

The operator was standing at the wellhead waiting to open the valve, but the tee and valve blew apart. The piece of steel that blew out went under his arm, and we never found that big chunk of steel.

I loaded up the top of the burner onto the hot oiler, tied it down, and headed back to Airdrie. The job was never done that day.

I arrived back at the yard determined to quit this job. I parked the hot oiler in the far corner of the yard and went into the office to announce my resignation to Jim and Bob.

Jim was apologetic after I told him of my near miss. Bob didn't say much and left Jim and me to sort it out.

Finally, Jim said, "What will talk you into staying?"

I said, "A new truck with a 3.5-million-diesel fired burner."

Jim got on the phone to see about getting a burner from Robinson's Oilfield in Calgary. They got a burner coming from Houston, Texas, and we started to design a new hot oiler.

This was the beginning of my future.

I was left alone to build this unit. I went to Calgary every day to help Rice Machine put this hot oiler together.

A Mack truck with a triplex transmission and a four-speed spicer behind that gave me sixty gears. This made for speed, power, and a wide range for any driving conditions.

I loved this truck and knew it inside and out because I was there while it was being built. It was painted blue and white, and I was proud as if it was my own.

For three years, I ran this truck and established a sort of reputation for doing a good job.

Miller had many men, but he had a solid nucleus of good men who stayed with him for a long time. These men made Miller money, and he appreciated them. He treated everyone fairly and favored no particular man.

He just asked for a certain dedication and to be on time for each job. We all respected that.

Al Lawther was Bob Miller's accountant/bookkeeper. He was quiet, hardworking, knew numbers, and how to make the numbers work to make a profit. Nothing was ever done without Bob's final approval. If you wanted a raise, it was only through him.

Financially Bob Miller and Jim Pagan treated me as well as they could, and I did very well.

One of the men became a good friend. His name was Dave Argent, and we were the same age.

Dave was a rodeo man. He loved to ride, and he knew animals very well.

He drove truck for Miller not because he loved it but because he needed to support his cowboy lifestyle. He rented some land and lived outside of Cremona in the hills. He was a great truck driver and taught me things about trucks that I would appreciate later on.

We traveled together. He was my nurse truck with his tank truck. He hauled me oil, water, and condensate. I heated and pumped the fluid for these jobs as they came up.

We went together to Crowsnest Pass from Airdrie to work on deep wells of Coseka Resources. These wells were high up in the mountains above Coleman.

We left the night before loaded with carbon disulfide on my hot oiler and condensate in his tank truck.

We got a room in Coleman to stay overnight so that we could be on the lease high above Coleman early in the morning.

This was like a holiday for Dave and me.

We checked in and hit the bar. The waitress got to know us, and we always shut the bar down and found a party after.

The next day we were hung over, but we were always on time and performed our job.

This job was very dangerous in the fact that the pressure of the well was extremely high.

The CS2 (carbon disulfide) was very volatile, and the automatic ignition point was 212 degrees Fahrenheit. This was critical, and we were extremely aware of that fact. This CS2 was for dissolving the sulfur plugs in the wellbore, and the condensate was pumped behind it to chase the chemical down the 15,000-feet wellbore.

The natural pressure of the well would push this mixture back to surface, and we would flow it into Dave's tank truck, salvaging the condensate.

The CS2 was spent, and we would send it to the flare stack to burn in the atmosphere.

Dangerous? You betcha.

We were living on the edge on this job, but Dave and I were confident and performed this job many times.

One day, however, we traveled to this one particular well, where we were met by an ERCB government inspector. He just wanted to see what this procedure was all about. He sat in his car watching while we did the job.

Flowing back the well, the choke we were using to control the flow of the well failed, and we directed the condensate and the CS2 prematurely to the flare and extinguished it.

This fluid overflowed the high stack and ran down. There was no fire, so just liquid was running down the stack. No fire! *Good*, we thought.

However, the CS2 ignited, being flammable at 212 degrees Fahrenheit. Everything caught fire down the flare stack and around it.

Every color was displayed in the fire, and the heat was immense. The flare stack was erected 150 feet from the well, so we were safe.

The tank truck hatch had blown off, and the condensate had run over the top onto the ground.

The miracle was that nothing caught on fire except the flare stack.

We were lucky—very lucky.

The ERCB was nowhere to be found. He drove away and was not heard from until three weeks later, when Coseka Resources was informed that our procedure of de-sulfuring these wells was finished.

The trips to the Crowsnest Pass were over for Dave and me.

# CHAPTER 23

# I'm Pregnant

During the career change that I was making from seismic animal to oil/gas well servicing, there was another change taking place, a change of life in every way for Sharon and me.

This one memorable day I walked into our little apartment in Calgary, and Sharon, still in her work clothes, was lying on the bed crying.

I stood beside her and asked what the problem was. Many things were going through my mind, but I had no idea what she was about to say next.

"I'm pregnant!" she exclaimed amidst sobs and tears.

I was happy. I grinned from ear to ear and said, "Oh good."

This was not in our plans. This was unexpected, and we could hardly afford to start a family. Not only the affordability, but the career Sharon had planned on was over. The promotion she had just received at Cominco now meant nothing. We would be a one-salary family, and Sharon's career would be mother and wife.

We both firmly believed in stay-at-home parenting, and that was our belief if we had kids. We had discussed this many times in the past. However, I was extremely happy, and I was already looking forward to the birth of our new baby.

For some reason I wanted a girl first. Why? I have no idea. Maybe it was because of my family, since the girls came first, and that was Lois, my sister. Maybe I was trying to recreate my own family in my design.

Sharon's doctor was a fantastic Nigerian doctor by the name of Smart-Abbey. He was one of the best there was in Calgary at that time. This was in 1973, and healthcare was still personal and the doctor-to-patient relationship was special.

We went through the prenatal classes, the mood changes, the calls to Sharon's mother, and of course, Granny.

During the pregnancy period, I was also learning my new job. Now this job became important. I was the sole wage earner because Sharon quit working at Cominco.

I couldn't just up and quit if things weren't going my way. Sometimes I would get very frustrated because I was still having withdrawal feelings from leaving the seismograph industry, where I had a lot of freedom and less responsibility.

However, I stuck with the job, and things became more interesting as I got more experience. The paycheck got better too. I became one of the highest paid at Miller when I became more valuable to them.

During the pregnancy period, we made two significant changes: Sharon quit her job and we moved to Crossfield, where a house was available for rent. This made things easier for work and gave us a small town atmosphere where we could meet people, and being from small towns, we missed this slower-paced life.

Crossfield was a growing community just off the busy #2 highway between Calgary and Edmonton. Being situated only thirty miles from Calgary, we had close proximity to the city services. This was helpful during the pregnancy, as Doctor Smart-Abbey was only minutes away.

We made many friends in Crossfield, and two were special to us. One was my boss's wife, Sheila Pagan. She couldn't do enough for us and helped Sharon immensely. She was a caring person. She cared about older people and children and was a creative housekeeper.

Jim and Sheila had two children, Andy and Kim. Our lives became intertwined because of work and similar lifestyles. We only lived down the street from each other, and things were good.

Another family across the street was the Linklaters. Lyle was a telephone worker for Alberta Government Telephones, while Joan was also a stay-at-home mom. They had three children: two boys and a girl. Lyle was an avid outdoorsman who was into hunting, fishing, and boating. He was also a handy-type guy in carpentry, masonry, and yard work, and he became a good friend.

Joan was perfect for Sharon at this stage. She'd been through the pregnancy part, and she was comforting to have as a neighbor.

These four people—Jim, Sheila, Lyle, and Joan—were a very big part of our lives at this point.

I was happy to work, become a dad, be married, and be with friends.

Life was good. Life was simple as it should be.

# CHAPTER 24

## It's a Boy

The spring of 1973 came and went. We had moved into our house in Crossfield, I was progressing at work, and we made new friends and adjusted to the small town life.

Summer began, and soon the final stages of the nine months required to create a new life were upon us. July was the due date; of course, this became two weeks overdue. July first became July fifteenth. That day, however, was for real, and away we went to the Holy Cross Hospital in Calgary.

Doctor Smart-Abbey was waiting, and the labor pains continued for twenty-three hours.

I was not allowed to be present during birth, as this was a Catholic hospital. This policy hadn't changed yet. So I waited in the waiting room, and waited, and waited.

Finally our baby was born, and I was presented with a son. I was a little disappointed that it wasn't a girl, but not for long.

A boy was fine, and we had a name picked either way. Timothy Ronald was the name we chose.

We were proud parents coming out of the hospital. After twenty-three hours of hard labor, Sharon was very happy to have that part over.

While Sharon was recovering, I was performing the easy part of notifying everyone I could think of that I was a dad now. The Beres family was first, of course. Bill and Jean, Sharon's parents, were now first-time grandparents. How exited they were. Granny Kalscits was beside herself with joy as she was getting on in years but not ambition. She made afghans, quilts, and clothes, and baby

Tim was on his way to being spoiled rotten by my family far away in Lestock, Saskatchewan.

This was fine by me because although we were poor, when we were kids family was always important, and a new baby was a special deal. I understood everyone's excitement.

There were doubts in my mind, however. Was I going to fulfill my duties as a dad? I thought back many times to the only role model I had, and I prayed that I wouldn't be like Daddy Heck, as I called him.

I had reason for these fears. I knew I had a drinking problem, and I had trouble behind me. I was afraid of the trouble that lay ahead, and little did I know then that there would be big problems to overcome.

The next year or two involved working and moving from one house to another within the town of Crossfield to try and scrape by on one income, because Sharon didn't work again. I insisted she stay home to raise the kids. Stay home she did, and this was hard for her. She missed her work and friends. She became a great mother from the start, became a good cook and housekeeper, and made friends easily. She adjusted to parenting much better than I did. I did my part though, and work was number one, as always. I was progressing quite well at Bob Miller's as a Hot Oiler operator and on much mechanical repairing because these types of trucks are prone to breakdowns. I learned a lot during my years with Miller.

I was guided very well by Jim and Bob.

As I said before, Jim Pagan's wife, Sheila, was a great help to Sharon, and a substitute mother/godmother. She was what Sharon needed at that time.

I was gone long hours on jobs that are sometimes far away. I was drinking at this time, but I figured I had pretty good control of it. I thought I could handle the drinking without the help of Alcoholics Anonymous. Oh, how wrong was I.

These intermittent drinking turned into binge drinking later, which I could have prevented, but hindsight is 20/20.

In 1974 Sharon became pregnant again. This one was planned, and we waited for the necessary period. I hoped for a girl, and I was hoping so bad that I would have bet anything that this one was a girl as I had hoped for on the first go-around.

Nope! It was a boy. I was pissed off again.

Now why I wanted a girl so bad I have no idea. Maybe it was because I had three sisters and they were easy to manipulate. Whatever the reason was, a boy was given by God. Take it or leave it.

We named him *Jeremy Robert* or *JR*. These names were changed by his friends later to *Jay*.

Tim liked Jeremy; he wasn't jealous of the new baby being around. Later on, he used Jeremy as a punching bag, a brother he could kick the shit out of if he wasn't caught.

However, Jeremy was quicker than Tim mentally and outsmarted him constantly. This was to Jeremy's benefit, and I quite admired the way he handled himself. Nobody got the best of him for long.

Jeremy was smaller than the other kids his age, but his good-natured, mental quickness gained him a lot of ground.

I became attached to him because he was a lot like me. He had a quick response, and we got a charge out of his wittiness. To this day, that character trait exists.

# CHAPTER 25

## Let's Go For Three

So we had two boys, Tim and Jeremy, but I dearly wanted a girl. I talked Sharon into getting pregnant again; only this time, I knew I was not going to get disappointed by thinking of a baby girl. I knew I, would be brokenhearted if the third one was a boy.

Let it happen. We'll just hope, I thought.

Tim was born in July 1973, Jeremy in April 1975, and Jennifer Anne in September 1976. I was so happy that I had my girl finally.

I bet Dave Argent, my work buddy that I traveled to Crowsnest Pass, with a Texas Mickey that Sharon would have a girl, and he paid up.

We had a bottle of whiskey by that time and proceeded to get very, very drunk that night.

This completed our family. I had the vasectomy after Jennifer was born. Had she been born second there would have been no Jeremy. That would have been wrong. Funny how life goes.

In 1975 before Jennifer was born, we were living in Carstairs, Alberta, of course, where we had bought a lot in town and put up a modular home.

I worked my ass off on this project and learned a lot about regulations, rules, taxes, and ownership of a house.

The town inspector was at our house constantly with a longer list of things to change for this code or that. Finally, I got mad and told him to fuck off and get out and that he was stepping way out of line because our home had already been inspected at Standoff, where they built it.

The Kinai Indian band had a building project where they were turning out modular homes by the dozens.

This inspector was inspecting stuff that had already been passed. He came back with the permit, and we were good to go. I guess he was either afraid of me or maybe he was looking for a kickback. Whatever!

We finished the basement to the best of my limited abilities as a carpenter. We were sitting around on a cold January night. It was storming big time. We were reading the Carstairs paper and came upon an advertisement stating that there was thirteen acres with an older house, a garden, raspberry bushes, and strawberries. The location was three miles east of Carstairs bordering the #2 highway between Calgary and Edmonton.

"Holy shit," I said to Sharon. "Let's go look at this place."

"No way," Sharon said.

"Come on, Sharon. It's not that bad out."

The phone call I made changed our lives forever. I phoned the guy, and he said that there were seven ahead of me, but the storm was preventing them from coming out from Calgary to look. He said that if I could get there and look at the place that I could buy it.

Away we went with the two boys bundled up, and we put in the deposit on $63,000 that he wanted.

"Great," Sharon said after we left. "How the hell are we going to pull this off?"

"Oh shit," I said. "Don't worry. We'll pull it off."

I wasn't sure about that, but I had a good feeling. I was right, and our modular home in Carstairs was sold right away and we bought the acreage east of Carstairs.

Sharon lost her new house, but we had thirteen acres with a big old house with character. I had lots of work to do now, but I was happy. I was out of town, no neighbors within spitting distance, and lots of room to park my hot oiler. Life was getting better.

Spring came and we had a big garden. One of the guys I worked with by the name of Lefty Walsh had a wife that became friends with Sharon. She figured chickens would be good to raise. We went 50/50 on 250 chickens. I fed those chickens, and they grew so fast and big that we were butchering and selling chickens in no time.

The only thing was that Sharon and I did all the work. We butchered them all in one day and I couldn't eat chicken for a year after the massacre.

Never again did we have chickens.

One day I was tilling the garden, admiring the acreage, and loving the moment. Lefty came over to bullshit on a slow Saturday. We were sitting at the table having a beer at about noon so we figured we would barbeque some steaks.

I went outside to start the briquettes. It had rained the night before, and the sand was wet that the briquettes lay on. I poured a little methanol from a five-gallon plastic jug I had for that purpose. I went back out after a few minutes to check and felt the briquettes. They were cold.

"Shit," I said. I picked up the jug and splashed some more on the coals to fire them again. I didn't know there was fire enough to light the methanol. Everything exploded, and I was rolling on the grass of fire.

Tim and Jeremy were with me playing and watching. Sharon's sister, Debbie, had come to Carstairs to stay with Sharon and help because Sharon was due to have the baby.

Debbie was also by my side when I lit up like a torch. She ran around the house three times before she found the door to get Sharon. Debbie was panicking and very scared.

Jeremy was just walking and thought this was pretty cool. He was dancing on the grass that was on fire.

Tim ran away, and I was rolling on the freshly tilled garden to put the fire out on my body from the waist up.

This was a mistake, but I didn't care. The doctor later said that infection can easily set in if you have dirt in a burn. He also said that the dirt would have to be removed. The blisters that came quickly were broken, and a nailbrush and morphine did the rest.

That was the most excruciating pain I had ever experienced.

This doctor in Didsbury looked after me all weekend. He would not let me go to the hospital in Calgary because he said that it was a weekend and that all that were on-call were interns, which wouldn't be good. He kept me until Monday, when Dr. Birdsell, the top plastic surgeon and burn specialist, was there at the Foothills Hospital in Calgary.

I'll always thank that small town doctor for that. He was a war veteran doctor who had looked after hundreds of severe burns in WWII.

Dr. Birdsell was the best, and the Foothills Burn Unit is still the best in Canada. I was lucky to have received excellent care.

Burns are mentally trying as well as painful. Nurses are picked for their attitude and compassion to work with burned patients.

Three weeks in intensive hospital care and a lot of other more severely burned people with me in that ward made me realize how lucky I was. Many were burned beyond recognition.

A young boy and a biker were the worst, and I felt their agonizing pain. The biker had been into drugs so heavily that none of the drugs they prescribed were strong enough to take his pain away.

Every day I was loaded onto a rubber stretcher and taken to a pool where they would cut the dead skin off my body, face, and hands and re-bandage me with loose bandages and silver oxide cream.

Sharon was nine months pregnant when this occurred. Needless to say, she was not on time because of the trauma I was in or maybe because she was late twice before.

I was still in the hospital when Sharon went into labor. I wasn't ready to be released yet, but I felt good enough and wanted to be with her when she had the baby.

This time I was going to be allowed to watch the baby being born.

I had a good relationship with all the nurses on the burn floor. It was about ten o'clock at night, and I begged them to let me go.

Finally they got together and said okay and that if I could bandage myself and do it right I could go with Sharon.

I did, and I promised I would buy them pizza and beer when they got off at midnight. They let me out, and I fulfilled my promise/bribe.

Sharon had been in and out of labor, so we went back to our acreage.

Her granny and Debbie were staying to help us through this crisis. It was a good thing too; we needed all the help we could get.

Finally, the labor came for real.

Off we went to Calgary. The Holy Cross was waiting to deliver my daughter, Jennifer. I was so happy that the pain of being burned was minor.

Life was good again.

# CHAPTER 26

## Stepping off the Diving Board

During my stay in the hospital recovering from my burns to my face, arms, hands, and chest, I had much time to think about my past, future, and present.

I developed a fear of fire, and I wasn't sure I wanted to return to the job of running a hot oiler unit for Miller. This was a tough decision because I loved the job and I was getting really good at it.

The fire aspect is what hot oiling is all about, and 3.5 million Btu per hour of flame created by atomized diesel fuel is a lot of fire. I was having visions of being burned again, and I decided to do something different.

I went into Miller's office after I got well enough and broke the news that I wouldn't be returning. Jim understood, but Bob was a little pissed. He said, "I thought Jim said you were a good man. You're not!"

I took that to heart, but I felt afraid and maybe I was being a baby, but I also felt I could do something on my own.

This fear of fire and Miller's push with his statement that day gave me an obsessive desire to start up an oilfield maintenance company called McGregor Oilfield Maintenance Ltd.

This was accomplished by Sharon and I having long talks about financing, which meant selling the acreage we both loved and putting everything into the business. This also meant renting again and giving up ownership. Sharon had given up her new house in Carstairs, and now she would give up her big old house on thirteen acres of land. For what? A used one-ton Ford truck with gin poles, empty toolboxes, and a dream?

But she must have believed in me because she was by my side in Olds when we walked into Burgess Fullerton's office at the Ford dealership to buy this truck.

He was overwhelmed by our appearance. Sharon was over nine months pregnant, and I was bandaged up from the burns.

He felt sorry for us, I think, and gave us what I thought was a low ball price of $28,000.

The truck was in good shape, and we put a down payment on it.

We went to the real estate and bank, where we arranged to sell the acreage, and the bank gave us interim financing to purchase the truck based on equity for the acreage.

We sold the acreage in no time and moved to Crossfield *again*! I hardly slept because I was afraid of failure. I wasn't sure of what I was getting into, and I didn't even know how to set the gin poles up. I was too proud to ask anyone. So Sharon and I practiced putting them up and down.

This must have been quite a sight, she being nine months pregnant and I hardly able to bend at the waist.

But we did what we had to do, and I sold myself to anyone who needed work done in the oil patch.

One of these customers was Carl Wood.

Carl was the most ambitious man I had ever met. He was not educated by way of schooling, but he had a degree in experience. He was originally from Manitoba and had started in the oilfields there. He had followed the oil activity west to Alberta, and everyone he met along the way taught him new things that he never forgot.

He had a fantastic memory, and numbers were his domain. He needed no calculator or computer. Most figuring was in his head, and the final results were put on paper. He had an amazing mind.

I respected and admired him. He was my mentor. I learned and listened to him.

Carl was contract-operating forty-five wells for various oil companies around Calgary, Airdrie, Crossfield, and Carstairs. He needed someone he could count on to do maintenance, construction, and hauling for his wells that constantly needed work.

I was the ticket. I wasn't tied down with any big outfit yet so I could do whatever whenever.

Carl had one other quality necessary in business: greed! He was very fond of money, and he was very good at making and keeping it. Taxes were his nemesis. He hated taxes and did many things to circumvent these tax problems. He was always within the law, however, but he found every loophole there was to escape the taxman.

He loved the hotel business. He had owned the Carstairs Hotel at one time and made big success from the business then sold it out for a handsome profit.

He owned land and lived in a house on a one-half section east of Carstairs. He owned a hay-stacking business, which custom-stacked hay for farmers. Custom baling and stacking was a good business for him. He could go twenty-four hours a day and did more in one day than most could do in a week.

Carl knew the big money was in contract-operating oil and gas wells. He always looked after every well and kept them running to make money for the owners of the wells. He always looked up to the rich oilmen that he worked for, and he got along with both the rich and poor.

He was a likable man and was in every walk of life. He belonged to clubs, donated to charities, helped down and outers, and stood up to the bullies and people who pissed him off.

His wife, Beth, was his main employee. She did everything: all of the house chores, parts running, and starting pump jacks engines that he couldn't get to. She checked wells, did banking, answered phones, and of course, drove him home if he got too drunk to drive from the hotel when he would sometimes overindulge while visiting his friends at the bar in Crossfield or Carstairs.

He was not going to lose his license and had an uncanny sense of knowing when he was over the line.

These were Carl and Beth Wood. They were about twelve years older than Sharon and me. We got along great. They were like parents to us. They talked, and we listened. I had ambition, dreams, and very little money. Carl had ambition, dreams, and a lot of money. Besides having money, Carl had experience and contacts. I saw this and used it to my advantage.

I worked hard for Carl on the many little jobs that he gave me, and I would work at any time—weekends, nights, or holidays. He appreciated that, and I needed the work to make my business pay.

# CHAPTER 27

# I Need Help

I couldn't do all the work myself, and Sharon was busy with three small children so she hardly had time to help me.

I phoned my nephew, Steve Piechotta, in Gull Lake, Saskatchewan.

He was unemployed and willing to work for me. He came to Crossfield to stay with us and work for me.

This was great! He was lots of fun to work with, and he learned as we went. We figured things out together and had our fair share of arguments, but all in all we worked well together.

One man wasn't enough, however, so Sharon's brother Keith Beres from Lestock, Saskatchewan entered.

Keith was a farm boy and was used to hard work and very little money. He was eager to make some serious money.

This was my crew. We all got along well together and worked hard.

Amoco Canada needed a crew like ours to construct a facility along Highway 2 between Edmonton and Calgary at Crossfield.

We got the job and worked eight hours per day, five days a week.

The other hours were spent working for Carl Woods on his wells. We put in lots of hours for a year.

After one year, things slowed down, and Keith and Steve went back home to Saskatchewan to pursue their lives as they had left them to come to Alberta to work for Sharon and me.

If you ever were to ask them, I'm sure they would tell you that the one year they spent with us embedded a seed of desire to someday return again to the oil money of Alberta's famous boom/bust cycles.

Anyone who has ever worked in the oil patch knows the saying, "Lord, give me another oil boom, and I'll promise not to piss it away this time."

Such is the way for many farm boys from Saskatchewan, and very few fulfilled this promise.

Keith and Steve were going to return again and again to pursue the promise.

I felt I had let them down, however, and there was something more out there in my future. I wasn't sure at this time, but I promised I would hire them back someday.

I didn't know then what I was going to do to accomplish this, but I had a strong feeling that I wasn't done hiring people. Oh, how right I was.

One slow day after Keith and Steve were gone and I was contemplating what my next job would be with my little one-man one-truck operation, my old buddy Harvey Watson phoned from Three Hills, Alberta. I had worked with Harvey on seismic at Pointed Mountain. He never forgot the joke I played on him about the girl with no legs in Toronto, and like that never-forgotten joke, our friendship remained intact. This would be the phone call that would be the major turning point not only in my life but in many, many others as well.

Harvey said, "Are you busy?"

I said, "Of course, not like you, dumb son of a bitch."

This was always the way with Harvey and me. We were always rude to each other, and we wouldn't have it any other way.

Harvey said, "Well, I've got a job if you want it. My ex-wife Jean bought a trailer in Didsbury, and she needs to have it skirted and set up in the trailer court. Tie in the septic and power and all that shit. Do you want to do that?"

"Sure," I said.

"Oh, by the way, there's a hot oil truck in Red Deer for sale," he said.

"Oh yah. What kind of piece of shit did you find now, Harvey?" I answered back.

"No," argued Harvey. "I think it is pretty nice from what this guy that owns it was telling me."

"How much?" I asked.

"Sixty-four thousand is their bottom line."

"Well, that's just about sixty-four thousand more than I got," I said.

"Maybe we should go look at it," Harvey said.

"Maybe I'll think about it," I said.

I did the job Harvey wanted me to do for Jean, his ex wife, and I couldn't get this hot oiler off my mind. Finally I told Harvey that I want to see this truck in Red Deer.

I had mixed emotions about this decision to even look at this truck. I had promised Sharon and myself that I was never going to hot-oiling again after my stay in the hospital.

This was why I had quit Bob Millar, and this was why I started the maintenance/construction business.

*Oh well, a trip to Red Deer wouldn't hurt,* I thought. This was probably nothing, anyway.

Oh how wrong I was.

Harvey and I went together and met with one of the owners of this hot oil truck.

Dan Kanudson was his name. He was partners with another guy named Ron. They were consultant engineers and thought that this would be a good deal to fit in with their consulting work. They were wrong because the dedication required in running this type of truck required much more at that time. And Harvey's partner was Ron Toews, who was quite a guy and loved to party and drink. I had a few sessions with him, and Sharon hated Three Hills and the party thing. I knew that a partnership between Harvey, Ron, and me wouldn't work for her.

Harvey didn't know the hot oil business, but he trusted me to know if we could make money with it. I assured him that there was money to be made but that it would have to be situated in Olds.

That wouldn't work, and Harvey wanted the truck in Three Hills.

There were differences and Sharon prevented the partnership from happening that spring of 1977.

Who knows what could have happened had we pursued this venture? Hindsight is 20/20, but we will never know.

At this time I was still doing jobs for Carl Wood, and I talked to Carl about this hot oil truck in Red Deer.

Carl was very interested, of course.

He was always interested in making money. I talked, and he listened. I was talking about how the truck was rigged up so far ahead of its time and how much work it could do, and Carl was adding up the numbers.

The numbers looked very good, but I knew I couldn't do it without a partner. Carl knew it too.

This was the perfect match. He had the resources, and I had the knowledge and experience of the hot oil business.

We went to the bank of Montreal, where Carl banked in Carstairs and I met the manager, Tom Swenson. Carl and Tom got along great, and I liked Tom too. Carl had dealings with Tom before and drank and partied with him.

Perfect, I thought. This should be easy.

Welcome to the banking industry. I was in for an eye opener. Bank managers don't have the stroke people think. They answer to Calgary and Toronto. The security has to be there. Many dreams are broken inside the bank managers' office.

I had my maintenance truck, some receivables, and a lot of ambition. Carl had plenty of money, land, and security.

I had one other attribute—stubborn in the fact that we would be 50/50 partners. That meant I would put up an equal amount of security and cash, and Carl would match that.

This was where we left it with the bank manager.

We needed a 10 percent cash down so the bank would finance the balance of the $64,000 truck.

We were also required $10,000 worth of operating/startup capital.

That night Carl phoned in. He said that Tom had called and said that the only way was for Carl to back everything up with a quarter of land as security.

I said, "No way!" The deal was off as far as I was concerned. I wasn't going in on the light end of a teeter-totter.

I held firmly, and Carl respected that.

I thought it was over, and I was discouraged in the fact that I was always a dollar short on cash and long on ambition. I was feeling sorry for myself when Carl came over the next day and said that Calgary told him that they didn't need the collateral of the land.

I was ecstatic. I later found out that Tom Swenson really stuck his neck out for us and painted a pretty picture for Carl and me to the bean counter in Calgary.

So we became true 50/50 partners—Carl, Beth, Sharon, and me—four people with four different backgrounds and four different personalities. We were all excited about this new venture.

Carl and I drove to Red Deer to look at this hot oiler and deal with the two consultants.

Carl was ready, but I knew that they were at the bottom dollar. They owed the same as what they wanted for the truck, and $64,000 was the bottom line.

We wrote the check, and they gave me the keys. I needed no training and drove away, feeling very proud and anxious to get back to Crossfield to get working.

I had a lot to do to start, and I was in a hurry to get things done.

We stopped at the Esso Restaurant on Gasoline Alley in Red Deer on the way out to have a bite to eat. We were sitting at the table looking out the window and the truck.

Carl said, "What are we going to call this outfit?"

I thought about it and looked at the gold and black block letters stuck on the door that said *Ronkan*.

I said, "Well, Carl, we can't afford much. So why don't we just buy four letters for each side and stick them on?"

"What letters?" Carl asked.

"W-o-o-d," I said. "We'll just call it Ronwood for now."

"Okay," said Carl.

The new name went on. The documents were drawn up for the company, and Ronwood Petroleum Services Ltd. was born on June 27, 1977. Oh, how sweet it was.

This was huge for me. I was into something I loved, and the Foothills Hospital and the memories of the fire and pain were distant and meaningless to me now. The future was the only thing I was concerned about now.

I quickly developed strength and a never-give-an-inch attitude.

This deal between Carl and me created a division between Jim and Sheila Pagan and Sharon and me. We were never close after this deal with Carl and Beth Wood.

Bob Miller's hot oiler was still active at this time, and Miller was our competition.

Carl looked after forty-five wells and utilized a hot oiler to dewax some of his wells.

I had worked for Carl many times when I was running Miller's hot oiler.

This work was now ours. This was not conflict of interest because Carl was contract-operating. However, the advantage was ours.

Carl did some badmouthing about Miller in the bar in Crossfield, and the word got around to Jim and Sheila.

We were not popular around the Miller crowd, and this weighed heavily on my mind.

But I knew I couldn't have it both ways.

I knew that there was too much friction in the small town of Crossfield and not enough work to go around for Miller and Ronwood.

Olds was looking pretty good at this time, and we rented a duplex and a shop to put the hot oiler in.

# CHAPTER 28

## Adjustments, Desires, and Blind Ambition

We had major adjustments to make when we moved to Olds.

These adjustments weren't easy for Sharon, I'm sure, although you wouldn't hear her whine and bitch like a lot of others would have. Instead of complaining, she dove into whatever had to be done and worked her ass off to try and make my dreams come true. This was the start of Ronwood, and without Sharon's sweat and hidden tears, I'm sure we would have failed early as so many small businesses do.

A huge adjustment was looking after our three kids. Our saving grace here was the duplex bordered onto a playground fenced and easily watched from our balcony.

We were handy to downtown Olds, and most of our shopping needs were met locally.

Sharon was an excellent driver, and she got around very well in whatever vehicle we had, which were many different makes and styles—fast cars, pickups, station wagons, big cars and little cars—she drove them all.

Sharon's number one thing was the kids and home, next was Ronwood. This meant invoicing, booking, answering phones, running parts, meeting customers, and being nice to people she would rather strangle.

This may seem easy in a one-truck operation, but dealing with oil companies and the nature of the hot oil business were not easy.

Calls came at any time of the day or night. We could be in bed at one in the morning and a call would come. I would be on the road with lunch, coffee, and clean working clothes, thanks to Sharon. I wonder now how she did it, but at that time, I figured this was the way everyone operated.

We had a lot on the line now: a family, a business, partners, debt, and hope for a house of our own someday.

It was a desire to achieve more to prove we could take advantage of this opportunity given to us that I knew could lead to bigger and better things if we did all right. I had a dream.

All I had to do was make it come true without turning the dream into a nightmare.

The nightmares were ahead, but the dream would last.

# CHAPTER 29

## Jobs, Jobs, and Jobs

This was what we were all about. Never turn a job down, stack them up, and book anything and everything. Talk the customer into doing tomorrow what he wants to do today. Sharon and I got really good at this trick. At times, we would have worked stacked up for two weeks without missing one job.

We were fortunate to have found a shop for the hot oiler close to our duplex. This shop had two bays because we knew that the second truck would have to be built. One truck wouldn't be able to handle the busy times and a breakdown was inevitable.

A shop was important to be able to withstand the cold and to work on the equipment.

Carl saw the opportunity and bought the shop. He leased it back to Ronwood. This was cool with me because I didn't want to tie up money in the long term and the rent was 100 percent tax write-off. The deal was made, and Ronwood had a home as long as Carl was a partner.

One night while we were sleeping at around two in the morning, the Ronwood phone rang. I gently nudged Sharon off the edge of the bed to answer. For some reason she was always pissed off whenever I did this, but she always answered with a sweet "Good morning, Ronwood."

This time the call was from Bert Veragus from Shell Oil.

Sharon happily said, "I think you'd better talk to Ron. He's right here." This was when she smiled at me because she knew I was going to work and she was going back to bed.

I didn't know Bert, but I knew about him. He was an international engineer for Shell Oil and traveled worldwide solving problems of the most serious nature. He was topnotch.

Bert asked me if I had a hot oiler. "Yes," I said.

"I understand you work for Shell, and they speak highly of you."

I was proud to hear him say that, and I asked him what the problem was. He just asked if I could get to Jumping Pound West in Calgary right away and that he would fill me in when I got there.

I knew this was important so I packed a lunch. Jumping Pound Shell was about a two-hour drive from Olds.

I was fueled up and ready to go. So I fired up the Ford Louisville and headed for the hills.

Before I arrived on location, I passed a bunch of pumpers from Halliburton parked on a lease before the one I was going to. I wondered why they were parked there.

I found out when I got to the well I was going to work on.

As I was driving toward the well, all I could see was the tip of the derrick of a drilling rig. I wondered about that because very seldom we worked with drilling rigs unless they were stuck in the hole.

I was right about that part, but not in my wildest dreams did I know why.

As I came around the mountain to drive into the valley that the rig was spotted, I couldn't believe how much equipment was parked, running and waiting.

They had a path cleared for me to drive up beside the rig.

I went to the engineer's trailer to talk to Bert.

We shook hands, and Bert asked, "Can you heat methanol?"

I said, "Yes, I can, but only up to 120°F."

"That's good enough," Bert said. "We have a manifold set up, and we want you to heat methanol and pump it down the casing, bleed back, and pump down back and forth until we get some heat to melt the hydrate that's holding everything up.

"There's 5,000 PSI below the plug, and the ice is frozen to the tubing that we're running in the hole. As soon as the casing frees up, we have these Halliburton pumpers and tank trucks full of thirteen-pound mud to kill the well."

I looked up at the top of the derrick of the drilling rig and saw that they had chained the tubing. That was all that was holding the tubing because the BOPs and the blind rams were also frozen. They were also working on that with steam, but casing was the key. They had to be able to pump the casing full of mud.

I started pumping hot methanol, which is a dangerous commodity to heat with a hot oiler and even more dangerous to bleed back.

There was a Chinook wind blowing from the west toward Calgary, and this well had a high content of hydrogen sulfide gas. I knew that if this went south on this deal, the results could be catastrophic.

I pumped and heated for forty-two hours. They had a camp set up down the road, so I was well fed. The danger of the job kept me wide awake.

Finally, the plug slowly dispersed, and the pressure began to rise at my pump.

I was happy, Bert was happy, and the vice president of Shell Oil was extremely happy. I met him during the job when he flew out in a helicopter. I was famous for a couple of days. I loved it.

The irony of the situation at this time was that there was a wild well at Lodgepole near Drayton Valley, where Red Adair was at and another wild well east of Calgary at a place called Cessford being put out by Boots and Coots, which was owned by Red Adair's son-in-law. The experts were all tied up, and Shell was left alone if this well were to go wild.

This well would have made the other wells look like farts in the wind.

This successful venture for me was quite important.

Bert had a lot of stroke at Shell Oil, and the advertisement I got from him was far reaching. Ronwood was Shell's first call for our type of services.

I was fortunate to have had this job gone as well for me as it did. I was to come upon many more critical jobs in the future, but no job topped the importance of this Jumping Pound job and working with an engineer of this stature. I was feeling good.

# CHAPTER 30

## Shell Oil and Ronwood

The move from Carstairs to Olds happened in a hurry. Our belongings weren't all that much, but our moving vehicle was not exactly a moving van. A car and an old pickup made the trip many times up and down Highway 2.

While we were moving into the small duplex, we were visited by a contact I had made through Bob Miller. Alan Bjorsnik was his name—a great guy who worked for Shell Oil at Harmattan, a field twelve miles west of Olds. I had been out hot oiling there, but the proximity to Red Deer for hot oilers was easier for Shell to utilize services.

Alan asked what was going on when he saw me tripping between the truck and the duplex. I said, "Well, Al I just had to move a hot oiler to be closer than Red Deer."

He laughed and promised I would be real busy for Shell, who was the big guns in the area. He was right on with that statement. The next day, in fact, I was out at Shell-Harmattan.

The boss man at Shell was a guy by the name of Dave Gibbs. He was hard-nosed, a little arrogant, and very stubborn, with a "my way or the highway" attitude. I respected Dave and got along well with him. We were alike in many ways, and I suppose he respected me as well.

Dave came to Harmattan from Swan Hills, and as these high-position transfers usually work, he transferred some of the men from Swan Hills to Harmattan. Much like a hockey team, when the coach or manager is fired or moves on to another team, usually, some team players migrate also.

Mike Kosik and Jim Wyness were two of the first. Mike was awesome. He put work on my plate that sometimes I'm sure was not absolutely necessary, but he knew we were starting out, and this was his way of helping.

Mike was into sports with his kids who were older, but he was instrumental in getting me involved with the Olds sports scene. Baseball and hockey, that's all we cared about or talked about.

This was what I wanted—a good work environment and a good start in sports for my three kids—and life would be great. How good it was going to get I wasn't prepared for. Like the old saying goes, "be careful what you wish for."

Shell Oil wasn't the only one needing the service of a hot oil truck. Hudson's Bay Oil and Gas, Andex Oil, and Canadian Superior were three big players in the area. There were warnings from people I spoke with along the way.

These warnings were as follows:

You'll never satisfy two of the biggest assholes in this area. These two assholes' names were Slim Kalis and Oscar Bennet. Slim looked after the east side of #2 highway, which is west of the Fourth Meridian, and Oscar was superintendent for everything west of #2 or west of the Fifth.

Both were drinkers, stubborn, and obstinate; and there were two ways: their way or no way. They had lots of power and stroke. They could make or break any small company like Ronwood.

They were both happy to see a hot oiler in the area because of the wax problems they had in a lot of wells at the time. They tried me out, and I passed the test because I was their first call.

Slim would be pissed if I was working for Shell, and he couldn't get me when he wanted. I promised him I would have more than one truck soon. This kept him on the line, and I did what I could to fit Hudson's Bay into my schedule.

The beauty of Shell Oil and Hudson's Bay Oil and Gas was that they paid by cheque for the job. Shell Oil foremen or supervisors had authority up to $1,000 and Hudson's Bay to $500. If the ticket was over that, then you made out two tickets. This helped us out immensely as we were struggling for cash. Cash was *king* for us. A buildup of cash meant better, bigger, and easier. Or so Carl said, and I believed capitalism stood for happiness. Or was it? We would soon find out.

Six months was all the time needed to find out that one hot oil unit was not going to be enough to handle the work coming our way. I worked my butt off, but we turned away more work than we could do.

The next move in our little chess game was to change my life forever.

# CHAPTER 31

## Priorities

Things were good at work; our rental duplex was adequate, with a community playground for a backyard. The shop was only two blocks away, and we were planning a second hot oil unit.

This is where I probably made the decision that I would live with forever.

Everyone I knew always said, "Family comes first, then work, then play." I did not agree with this philosophy. I felt work, business, money always came first.

I was brought up poor, and I always felt that if my dad had been successful, our family would have been much happier, leading to an easier path to a successful future. Life wouldn't have had to be so much of a struggle to get ahead.

I watched Carl Wood, my mentor/partner, and he always professed to be a "family first" man. I said to myself, "Bullshit." Carl ate, drank, and slept business. He started as poor as anyone, and work was his avenue to happiness. If work interfered with family, then work took precedence.

Holidays were cut short, weekends were nonexistent, and the only loyalty to a social life was the legion, which he took very seriously.

I knew where Carl's head was at, and I drew on that. Our three kids were in preschool when we started at Ronwood. We enjoyed them; but the commitment was small with diapers, bottles, and keeping them fed and healthy.

Sharon was an excellent mother/homemaker. She was adept at multitasking. Accounting books, answering the phone for business, shopping, doctoring, making new friends, and looking after me never seemed to be too much for her. Kindergarten, school, and sports were just around the corner; but I knew that she could handle all that in stride.

For me, my life revolved around work. My business was top priority, and that was the way it would remain.

I enjoyed the kids, played guitar, loved music, and partied when work allowed it. Partying and drinking were soon to be a problem, however, as time went on.

Whenever work would allow it, we would travel to Lestock, Saskatchewan, to Sharon's parent's farm. Bill and Jean would always love having the kids for even a weekend. This was an escape for me. Sharon's mother, Jean, would fuss over me; and I would relax and sleep. There was no pressure at their place. Theirs was a laid-back farm life, and whatever needed to be done could always wait a day or two.

Food, drinks, and a few laughs and stories made up the way of life in Lestock, Saskatchewan. This was good therapy for us, but only for a few days.

I couldn't wait to get back to Olds because I had to be missing something work related. We were still a one-truck operation, but I knew that we were not going to remain that way, and I knew what lay ahead.

# CHAPTER 32

## Cloning Hot Oilers: Headaches and How to Succeed in Business and Fail at Marriage

Oh, how true that **Chapter** title was. We went to our friendly banker in Carstairs again. Tom was very helpful this time. There was no land mentioned for collateral. All he requested was our books. That was easy. Sharon did our books, and the accountant was on the ball.

Our first six months surpassed every projection we had put forth on start-up. Everyone could see we needed more equipment. Our problem was our receivables—*always and forever.*

The oil companies, aside from Shell and Hudsons' Bay, were and still are famous for late pay, no pay, and "We'll pay when we want to." This is the biggest "piss off" in the oil patch for small companies.

One year a survey was done on this delay in pay, and the oil companies were estimated to have gained 45 million dollars from withholding payment over ninety days from service and supply companies.

This, to me, was, is, and will forever be chicken shit. There is no reason for it, and the card they play costs them money, but the little bean counters can't see this. Every slow-paying company we work in gets charged extra at the job site.

---

One prime example was Dome Petroleum. The Headman of Dome was a geologist and an excellent businessman. He turned Dome into a giant. He had a terrific personality, hence the nickname Smiling Jack.

Dome grew fast and bought up companies to gain land—on borrowed money of course. Shares escalated in value. Shareholders were ecstatic. Dome was the jewel in the energy industry, and Jack was the keeper of the jewel.

Nothing went by old Jack. One time he went for a walk in the Neutral Hills at Consort, Alberta. Being a geologist, he took note of the surface structure of the land and the soil changes. As he walked west of the Consort Gas Plant, he took note of the hills, the changes, and the distance from the gas field that Dome had discovered at Sounding Lake, where they had built a medium-sized plant and a pipeline network to sell natural gas. There was a lot of gas, but natural gas wasn't worth a lot. This meant a lot of production to make money.

Oil was different, oil was king of the patch, and everybody was looking for the black gold. Oil was going up because of OPEC, and believe me, OPEC made a lot of millionaires and billionaires in North America.

The Arabs didn't know it, but the more they jacked up the oil price, the richer American oil became. The glass towers in Calgary, Houston, and Dallas were not accidents. The Arabs had no idea whom they were benefiting in the big scheme of things.

Smiling Jack knew politics as well as geology. Money was his motivator, and geology was only a stepping-stone to power. As he was walking along the Neutral Hills, he was probably thinking about more than just rocks.

However, Jack walked about twenty miles and put a stake in the ground. This was where the oil started, he stated in a dramatic fashion. I was relayed this story by Dunn Magnesson, who was the superintendent of Dome in the Provost area. A tall ambitious, smart Norwegian, Dunn got things done. I suppose God knew that when he was named Dunn by his mother.

Dunn was very important to Jack, and Jack knew how to treat his employees—reward the ones that made Jack money. Dunn was rewarded, but not nearly what he was worth.

Dunn said that Jack's walk in the hills that day was only one mile off the discovery well that IPC Oil and Gas discovered twenty years later.

That, my friends, is phenomenal. Had Dome drilled when Jack proclaimed this and wildcatted, they would have hit the large oil field known as the Dina Zone. Sour black oil. Big money—*big returns*.

This is a story that meant a lot later on to Ronwood. But first, to show how Jack and some were in those early days, I had to relate how smart they were and how powerful they would become.

They were the worst for withholding payment as long as they could. This was thought of as cash flow backup. It's growing too fast, everyone figured, "Oh well, Dome is waiting for money, so we'll have to wait too." This theory is *bullshit*. Dome used us to gain money to show cash flow in their favor to the greedy shareholders.

These were the housewives, the stock players, the manipulators who never worked hard except to find their golf balls they had lost in their pitiful games, which they used to make deals and to figure out ways to screw the small guy out of any cash they could.

We became the proud owners of $65,000 of receivables from Dome. This was huge for us, but it was not just us. There were hundreds of companies in Alberta holding the bag for Dome.

Dome had purchased Hudson's Bay Oil and Gas. Hudson's Bay had the right to every section 8. This gave them free land to drill on, and believe me, section 8 meant a lot in a hot area. Dome knew it, and they had the government behind them.

They were the jewel, remember. Not to me, they weren't. They were a pain in my bank account. After ninety days, our receivables were stroked from the list, and Dome was nothing to our receivables. I would be told every day to add on to the invoice for late payment by the guys we worked for in the field.

After Dome bought Hudson's Bay, they ended the self-pay on location that helped us out before. I hated Dome for this, and many other companies like Czar Resources followed their example. Our receivables sucked big-time. Luckily, our banker was understanding in this scenario and rode the wave with us.

Tom Sveinson was awesome. He drank too much, but he was a working man's banker. Thank you, Tom, wherever you may be.

Tom came with Carl and me one day to see the hot oiler in action on a job. I was proud to show him what hot oiling was all about, and he was paying attention. This day was reflected to Calgary when we borrowed money, and it helped a little. Everything helped in our position.

We added the one hot oiler and then two more in short order. We were flying high. But oh well, as any businessman knows, there are money peaks and valleys. We were on a peak. The only problem was no one knew how tall the peak was.

We came sliding down the short peak into a valley that probably prevented us from becoming a major player in hot pressure and hot oil servicing.

The *infamous* National Energy Program came in, thanks to the intellectual asshole in Ottawa—at the time Pierre Elliot Trudeau.

I hate writing his name, but this name has been used in much anger by every right-winger in Canada and in some U.S. circles.

A communist-leaning prime minister was all we needed, and like it or not, we were stuck with this pompous asshole for a long time.

He hurt many companies, and we banded together under Elmer Knutson, who had started a political pressure group under the name of West Fed. Western Canada Federation was the name, and Elmer was at the helm.

We backed West Fed as did many other service and supply companies of the 1980s. Elmer's theory was simplistic, too simplistic perhaps. This theory was as follows: We are not a political party looking for control as a party running for election. We are only a pressure group. *God* knows there are enough parties out there and too many politicians.

What we need to do is put pressure on these people to do the right thing. Pressure the ones that can do the most good not only for us as individuals and companies but also for Western Canada.

The East has always controlled the West, and this will forever be until we make them pay attention.

I paid attention to this West Fed philosophy, and Elmer was bang on at that time, and today the same applies, although now it is too late.

The left-wingers have gone too far, and as everyone can see, the Eastern North Americans have sucked both countries into an abyss of debt we will never get out of.

Had more people paid attention to the West Fed philosophy, we would be in good shape today.

Hindsight is 20/20, and Elmer has passed on along with Trudeau.

Elmer was my mentor, and I helped in a small way, I hope. I was chairman of the Olds **Chapter** and helped organize meetings and round up support and media coverage. Thanks to Elmer, I had a perspective and an ideal to pursue in the future.

I also developed an attitude toward the rich oil companies, the government. and unions that I still hold today.

The saying I love best is by Winston Churchill: "Any man can face adversity. Give him power to show true character."

I saw this every day and still see this power abused everywhere. I've seen men developed from battery operations and good operators too. Operators made into foremen or supervisors who have turned power-seeking and abusive to their underlings. These people are more plentiful than you would want to think.

The list is long, but usually, their careers are shortened by fate.

# CHAPTER 33

## More Men, More Trucks, More Money

Truck 2 was a natural. Carl and I both knew this. Carl bought a used gravel truck, and we actually hauled some gravel with this truck before we stripped the box off and sold the box, hoist and hydraulic pump, and motor. This was a good buy.

The truck was cheap, which was a good beginning to building another hot oiler. I had experience in building a hot oiler from the Bob Miller days, but this time, I had a truck to copy from—the one that we had. Unit 1, which we probably called the first one, was a good example. The guy that built that truck knew what he was doing.

We cut corners, however, and kept costs down on the second truck. This trick would come back on us, but we got the truck on the road. Then the age-old problem arose: who are we going to hire to run this one?

I spent time at the tire shop called Wooton Tire in Olds. By this time, we had moved out of the duplex and bought a small house, two doors south of the tire shop. An affordable house, with a basement—ours and an investment to boot.

Brian Laviolette was the owner of the tire shop. A good friend he became to me. He liked to drink as much as he liked to make money, and he was good at both.

He had his nephew from Quebec working for him. His name was Robert Sauvé. He was French all right, but he spoke excellent English, and he had an awesome personality and sense of humor.

He was young, ambitious, and loved trucks. This was the guy I wanted, but he had no oil patch experience. I figured, "Good, then he's got no bad habits. I will teach him what he needs to know and train him to do what I want him to do my way."

Carl liked him right off the bat, mainly because Robert made Carl laugh, and they both got along well. I trained Robert on unit 1, and I started off the new one.

Life was good again, and Ronwood doubled in size in only six months.

The third hot oiler was not of necessity. This one was born of greed and ambition. More power, faster, fancier, and more money.

We wouldn't have the work to support three units in Olds, but that didn't matter—we knew we could put it to work somewhere.

This proved to be more difficult than we could have known at that time.

# CHAPTER 34

# Human Resources:
# Who Wants to Work?

Robert Sauve was my only employee when we started building unit 3.

Robert was into trucks; he knew more than Carl and me about what should be in a truck for power, transmission, and rear ends. Of course, a truck had to look good.

We shopped for this truck and bought the best Ford Louisville available at that time. Both Carl and I were believers in keeping the fleet the same to keep parts, service, and shop the same. This meant dealing a lot with the same shop personnel in the city.

We put more thought into designing this hot oiler, and it turned out very well.

The problem was working to keep it as busy as the other trucks. I had been doing work in Turner Valley, Black Diamond, and Waterton when I was with Bob Miller. They were now bringing trucks out of Red Deer to get proper service. I figured that High River and Black Diamond were good places to set up. The trick was living accommodations and a shop to put the hot oiler into.

We solved this when Robert purchased a trailer. We had to pay $3,000 up front for lot rental, which was huge for us at that point. We found a Quonset on a farm to rent for a shop, and I fixed up a 1971 Chevy pickup with new paint for Robert to drive. He was happy, we were happy, and away we went.

Who knew there would be a slowdown and that work was not plentiful? This was our first taste of a downturn.

Robert was excellent at touring around, looking for jobs, but the economics weren't good.

We got work, but every month resulted in a negative number. We were guaranteed salaries. So Robert was surviving, but like any trucker, he wanted to be busy.

Rachelle was Robert's wife. She was French like Robert, and they had two children. Being a good mother, she kept occupied, and they both socialized very well.

Robert was a great drinker in the sense that he could drink all night and you would never know. I envied him for that. I always showed my drinking, as most people do. Many times, I had to be helped home or nursed to semisoberness. Drinking to me was to get drunk, and the faster I drank, the faster I got drunk—trouble in the bottle.

Not so with Robert—he was calm, cool, and witty. He was and still is to this day the only employee that ever made me second-guess myself.

One year of slow time in High River was what it took to bring on the surge of activity that we needed. Economics changed. Turner Valley, Claresholm, Black Diamond, and Waterton all became active. One truck in High River wasn't enough. We were sending backup from Olds. Feast or famine, the way of the oil patch.

Soon, we were building a fourth truck and a pressure truck.

This was also the point when my brother Orville McGregor was laid off as a grader operator in Saskatchewan and took a mediocre job. I suggested he come to Olds to rig up a steam truck.

He came to Olds to check things out, liked what he saw, went back to Swift Current, and proceeded to move to Olds. We went out and bought a truck, a van, and a steamer. We put this together, and Orville worked hard to make this work.

We put him under Ronwood's name and insurance and charged a percentage. In other words, Carl and I got him started. Good deal both ways.

Orville had a narrow vision in the respect that he did his job, but socializing and getting involved in Ronwood or any promotional affairs was not his forte. We respected that and left him to his own devices.

I'm sure that twenty-five years of lonely grader operation and farmwork instilled a sense of independence and individuality.

We worked well together, and I bought a pressure wash outfit in Calgary that had a contract with Canadian Pacific Railroad (CPR) to clean coal and sulphur cars. This was to become invaluable to us in the slow times. We would clean out these hopper cars by the hundreds. We would give CPR a price per hopper car and go ahead and clean them by a certain time or date.

This was hard menial labor, but we would hire labor and get it done. Most of the time, we would do most of the work, but we felt good when we were alone. Orville and I worked well together.

Two more men were hired at this time. Jim Knapp and Joe Rinas both knew absolutely nothing about what we did or how anything worked. Great, I loved training people to do what I wanted them to do. No bad habits, so to speak.

These two were adversaries over a girl and were determined to do well at their job. This was a perfect storm for me. I wanted them to go out, work hard, and make me money.

Jim Knapp was a perfectionist. Everything had to work properly. He was not adverse to pouting and being a bit of a whiner. But he did his job well and was prompt, efficient, and related well with customers.
Joe Rinas was for Joe Rinas. The advantage was his. If there was a gain, he wanted to be part of it. This will show up later on.

Three more men were added to the mix at this stage. One of these men was Keith Beres, Sharon's brother, who had worked for me on McGregor Oilfield Maintenance at Crossfield/Carstairs. Sharon's sister, Debbie, was working on a short-term basis to earn some money to go to university. I taught her to drive a tank truck, and she got real good at it. Ironically, she trained Keith, her brother, to drive this ten-speed transmission.

Keith was a terrific employee. He had a great attitude—he was very mechanically inclined and was used to making things work from his farming experience, where he learned to do a lot with a little ingenuity.

Debbie stayed with us in the four-level split house we purchased when the house by Wooton Tire became too small. She was a great help with the kids and the house, and Sharon loved having her around.

Keith became good friends with the next employee I was to hire at this point.

Brian Laviolette was a relative of Robert Sauve, my hot oil operator. He came looking for a job one day, having had pressure truck experience up north. I wasn't a fan of hiring experience, but this guy looked good. Little did I know how intertwined our lives would become. He became more than just an employee later on.

This mix of people completed the Olds branch and Robert Suavé was established in High River, Alberta. All that was left was clear sailing—easy money. That is one of those "could have," "would have," "should have" situations.

What follows shows how a twist of fate can change any well-laid-out plans.

# CHAPTER 35

# Time for Hockey

By this time, the boys, Tim and Jeremy, were old enough to start playing sports. As with all boys that age, hockey was the game.

We started them off at an early age, around five years old, and away they went. They were hilarious to watch, and we knew it wouldn't be long before they would be skating, shooting, and hitting with the talents they developed with practice.

I would drive them out to Huber Dam just south of Olds; and if the ice froze before the snow came, there was nowhere better to learn to skate, shoot, and develop turning skills than a large span of ice like Huber Dam. You could skate one mile without turning back.

We loved it, but the snow would eventually come, and the ice would be covered. This brought back memories of when I was a kid and did the same thing. I would take a shovel to clear snow to expose the ice. This was a lot of work but well worth it.

The boys got their start in hockey early in life. Then Halloween 1978 came. The wind was up, and the brilliant teenagers of the day decided to light fires with diesel-soaked bales of hay all over Olds. I chased after a truck full when I came home from work, but to no avail.

That night a fire was set in the cow palace, as they called it, and spread to the grain elevators. After the fire got hold, the curling rink, the skating rink, twenty houses, and all the grain elevators were on fire.

There were seventy fire trucks/pumpers, helicopters, and water bombers. Ronwood even supplied a tank truck. Olds had no winter sports facilities after that. We used Didsbury, Bowden, and Sundre to practice and play.

In the ensuing two years, the drive was on to build a seven-million-dollar sports complex. This was accomplished through the governments, Town of Olds, and business and personal donations.

The community came together and accomplished a huge task. A man by the name of Burgess Fullerton was the drive behind this. He was a take-command influential person who also took a lot of criticism, which is normal for anyone who takes charge of public situations.

Burgess's son Bev was our welder whom we used at Ronwood, repairing and building. He did a lot of work for us. He too had two boys in hockey. We got to be very good friends through work and sports.

The Halloween fire in Olds was under Bob Armstrong's watch, who was mayor at the time. The fire not only produced a state-of-the-art facility in 1980 but also produced a 750 percent increase in business taxes for the town businesses.

The people of the town complained, but the wheels of progress were in motion. The complex was built, and the complaining still goes on today.

The main advantage the two years of rebuilding brought was an Alberta Junior Hockey Team called the Olds Grizzlys. This meant a high level of tier II hockey.

I got totally involved in the Grizzly organization. I became a director on the board and put Ronwood money into shares of the team.

We *billeted* players in our home. The first was Rory Delouise from Staten Island, New York. He was a goaltender with a flamboyant style. He was a wonderful young man, shy but aggressive in hockey. He was great around kids, and our kids loved him.

The other player we billeted was Gary Saloff from the Crowsnest Pass area. He was a defenseman and an enforcer. He loved to fight; and of course our boys, Tim and Jeremy, idolized him for his tough play.

These two were our main link to hockey at that time, and the introduction to the new Grizzlys in town was fantastic.

The next year we billeted a player from Vulcan, Alberta; his name was Darren Gorzitza, who was a talented player and a good scorer.

The fourth and last player was Darcy Wakaluk, another goaltender with a high ambition. Darcy was a terrific ambassador who was well liked by everyone.

His short life in Olds produced an NHL career; and he ended up with Buffalo, Dallas, and Phoenix, eventually going from player to coach. He deserved the glory of the NHL, and we were proud.

# CHAPTER 36

# We're the Government and We're Here to Help You

As the '70s rolled through and spawned the '80s, there was not only a new hockey team in Olds, there was something much more devastating developing. This was the National Energy Program. This program was set up by the Liberal government in Ottawa to equalize prices for oil and gas across Canada.

A tax scheme was set up by none other than Pierre Elliott Trudeau and Marc Lalonde.

This program was brought on by the Liberal philosophy that if you took more from the provinces that had more and redistributed the wealth to the have-not provinces, then life would be good for everyone.

This was purely political, and Western Canada knew it. Eastern Canada loved the program, and the majority of votes were in the east.

The fight was on. Peter Lougheed was Alberta's premier at this time, and he had the west and the oil industry behind him. His famous statement "Let the eastern bastards freeze in the dark" became the battle cry for us westerners. He also threatened to turn the tap off to the east for oil shipments.

Meanwhile, we organized as separatists. We felt the east was of no importance to the west. We had ports to ship from in British Columbia and

Manitoba. We could manufacture in Manitoba and Alberta, and of course we had the United States as a major customer for oil and gas.

Elmer Knutson was the founder of West Fed. This was not a political party but a pressure group designed to put pressure on the governments in power. This was much similar to the Tea Party. They would influence politicians to do what they promised to do while running for office.

I got heavily involved with this concept and felt that this was exactly what was needed to pressure Ottawa and their majority Liberal government to rewrite the National Energy Program.

Many service companies, supply companies, and small manufacturing companies were going bankrupt.

We had many meetings across Alberta and Saskatchewan to convince the people to join West Fed.

However, as usual, politics got in the way; and a party called Western Canada Concept was formulated. I never did agree with this idea, but another political party was thrust into action. I totally agreed with Elmer Knudson in that we did not need another bunch of politicians running around making promises they couldn't and wouldn't keep.

Five years of arguing and fighting over the National Energy Program sucked the advantage that the west had and put the western provinces into a deep recession. No one will ever know how much damage was done to the companies related to the oil industry; but this also prompted many outfits to move across the border to the United States. North Dakota, Montana, Oklahoma, Texas, and Wyoming gained a lot of Canadian expertise and equipment in these years.

Although Ronwood was a small player at this time, we felt there may be an advantage to move equipment south where there was less interference from government and the harder you worked, the more you were compensated. The United States was welcoming Canadian companies with open arms at this time.

My friend Harvey Watson felt the same way as we did. We went together to Tulsa, Oklahoma, to survey the situation for work for our trucks. Harvey had bed trucks and tank trucks. I had pressure trucks and hot oilers. We were short of work in Alberta, and trucks are easy to move to wherever the work might be.

We talked to friends of ours who had already moved to Oklahoma, and there was plenty of work. The risk was high if the U.S. work slowed down and things didn't quite look right. We backed out of this opportunity, and the future proved us right. We're happy we didn't move any equipment south of the border.

# CHAPTER 37

---

# The Devil Escapes from
# the Bottle (AGAIN)

So many times in my thirty-four years I fought with the effects of alcohol—my father's drinking and, later in life, my mother's. Only one member of our family of six would have no part of drinking—my sister Lois. She despised it and let everyone know that she despised drinking.

No one in our family could drink responsibly at one point or another in their lives. I was by far the worst of all.

I could very seldom drink for fun and leave it at that. I had to drink to get drunk. This is when the trouble usually came in the form of fights, accidents, police, jail, and afterward always remorse, guilt, and self-pity.

The alcohol problem was getting worse every year; and marrying, being a parent, having a business, and standing in the community did not alleviate the problem.

Several times I joined Alcoholics Anonymous to get help, but these times were short, and the honesty and resignation of being a person with a drinking problem was not sincere.

There were damages to my marriage, my business, and within myself that I was failing to see.

---

The trip to Oklahoma with Harvey Watson and Bob Clem was one of those situations where the drinking took precedence over the business at hand.

I proceeded to get very drunk but for the grace of God stayed out of serious trouble in the United States. When Harvey and Bob decided to turn in for the night, I decided to carry on at the nightclub we went to, all night. This was characteristic of the type of drinker I was. One was not enough. There was no counting when I was drinking.

The saying at the time when we were partying as seismic workers was "Bring one hundred and call the cops." This pretty well summed up the way I drank.

Back in Alberta, the drinking would start and stop. I was not a daily drinker, and sometimes several weeks would go by without drinking at all.

This is why AA was comfortable for me when I attended. I didn't have the addiction to drink all the time, making it easy for me to quit for short terms.

This is the dishonesty of my AA time. I knew what type of alcoholic I was, I just preferred not to seriously deal with the problem.

Carl Wood and Sharon, my wife, could not understand this part of me. They knew I had the problem, but they couldn't see why I couldn't deal with it.

Everyone was supportive, and I could con anyone into believing this particular time of trouble was the last time.

One of these times was after a spell of day and night drinking until I felt the only way to ease the pressure from everyone around me was to leave.

I ordered a charter plane from Skodopol in Olds. They arrived at my house; and I left for Kelowna, British Columbia, where my best friend Jack O'Connor was living.

The plane had a bar, and I drank nonstop during the trip. This was just another expensive drunk in my mind. My friend Jack nursed me back to sobriety and, after a few days, drove me home.

What I had waiting at home was not what I had expected.

A meeting was called with Carl and Beth Wood, 50 percent owners of Ronwood; Sharon, my wife; and our lawyer Steve Stiles from Carstairs who had set up our company.

The meeting was to remove me as president of the company and to remove me from managing. I wasn't happy, and I said so. I said, "Go ahead and run this outfit, but don't ask me for help—ever."

# CHAPTER 38

# I Needed Help

When I was twenty-one years old, I was in a terrible downslide from drinking too much, work pressure, and internal turmoil.

The seriousness of what had just happened at our board of directors meeting that led to my removal as president brought everything to ground level for me. I had to come to the realization that everything I had struggled to achieve was easy to lose. I was discovering that the fall from the ladder of success was much faster than the climb.

I had to make a decision, and this was to get professional help.

Through my time in Alcoholics Anonymous (AA) in the past, I knew about rehabilitation centers.

One of these was not far away. Located in the foothills of the Rocky Mountains of Alberta was Claresholm. Their rehab center was highly spoken of.

I was fortunate to be able to have access to their three-week program, and I decided to go to get help. I explained this to Sharon, my wife, and Carl, my partner.

They were both happy that I would seek professional help to straighten myself out. The seriousness of what I was doing to everyone around me was beginning to hit home.

I entered the program not knowing what to expect.

At first I felt I was in another institution, trapped and alone. This changed as I found that there were twenty other people with addictions that they were trying to work through to better themselves.

We worked as a group helping each other. Although we each had our own problems, we drew on each other to find out more about ourselves.

I worked hard at the program, and Sharon came to stay for one weekend.

I was happy to have found extended help. My personal counselor was a former nurse from Ponoka, Alberta. She had worked for many years as a psychiatric nurse in Alberta's most famous mental hospital, Ponoka Health Center.

When the program ended, we were all interviewed by our counselors.

My counselor, Ruth, interviewed me and finally said, "You are not an alcoholic." I thought, *Good, then why am I here, and where do I go now?*

Then the most profound statement I had ever heard—and probably ever will hear—was "You are a manic-depressive." I exclaimed, "Oh lovely, now I'm a maniac."

She laughed and said, "No, you're not a maniac, and your condition can be controlled."

After the initial shock of being diagnosed, I was now becoming very curious about what this manic-depressive thing was all about.

Ruth informed me that I had Dr. Reid as my family doctor in Didsbury, Alberta, and that they had worked together in Ponoka for many years.

She instructed me to make an appointment with Dr. Reid when I get home, and she also told me that he would start treating me for what was an incurable, yet very controllable condition.

I had faith in Ruth, and I trusted that what she told me was true.

I felt there was hope now; and I was uplifted knowing there was treatment available, although at this point, I don't know how much self-discipline there would have to be.

Sacrifices would have to be made, and it would be entirely up to me to make them.

My last night in rehab was confusing because I had no idea what the future held for me. A new diagnosis which I had never heard of. Would anyone believe this supposedly incurable condition that I supposedly inherited from my dear mother?

Many thoughts raced through my mind that last unforgettable night.

Another problem was stuck in my head from the time spent in Claresholm: one of the patients was found out to be *using* during rehab.

The solution to that problem was to put it to a vote by the other patients. Should he stay or go? was the simple question. We were to vote on with a simple show of hands. He was voted out of the program and was asked to leave.

He did leave, and within three days he was found dead in a park. He had overdosed, and word got back to Claresholm somehow. This weighed heavily on everyone's shoulders. I felt that this was too much responsibility to put on patients who were obviously having mental issues with their lives.

This issue stayed with me forever, and I tried to use this incident to guide me in the future. This worked for a time, but forever is a long time. The incident was in my memory, but it never affected my behavior when I most needed something to grab on to.

# CHAPTER 39

## The Best-Laid Plans of Mice and Men

The day of departure from rehab was a happy day for me.

Sharon, my good wife, picked me up; and we were looking forward to getting help with the manic-depressive problem.

I didn't know much yet, but I was determined to find out from dear old Dr. Reid.

I made the appointment and promptly showed up in his office.

He explained all about the condition. Yes, he knew all about Ruth in Claresholm. He had high regards for her. In fact, he didn't reassess me. He prescribed lithium and scheduled me to have blood tests done regularly to monitor the amount of lithium in my bloodstream (lithium can only be monitored through blood tests).

He also made two statements I wish now he never had made.

One was that I could casually drink in moderation. *Wrong!*

Another was that I would lose the condition in my fifties or sixties. *Wrong!*

These were huge mistakes. There can be no alcohol, and the condition never dies until the body dies.

I didn't know these two errors would haunt me in the future.

I was excited to start the program on lithium—lithium is not a drug, it is simply a mineral salt to level the mood swings. This was discovered in Roman times when the Romans would send troublesome people to a spa which had mineral baths. These baths contained lithium salt. After two or three weeks, they were sent back to Rome where they functioned normally until the next manic episode.

The lithium influence was not known at that time.

It was not tied together until the 1930s; manic depression was not known about very long when I found out about my condition. Now this is called bipolar disorder, because I think bipolar sounds much better than manic depression.

I bought books and studied—I really tried. I started back in AA, and I was reinstated as president and manager of Ronwood.

Everyone was happy to see me change for the better.

This was not to last, however.

An addiction is a powerful thing. This I developed long before being diagnosed as bipolar.

Things went relatively well at home and work.

The National Energy Program was behind us, work was picking up, the employees were getting well trained, and High River and Wainwright were turning into good moves until one day, Robert Sauvé gave notice that he was going back to Ontario.

This was not a bad thing. I just shut down High River and concentrated on Olds and Wainwright. The profit in High River never happened as we had hoped.

Robert was excellent as an operator, but expensive to maintain. I was somewhat pleased to see High River end. Joe Rivas in Wainwright was similar, but I had high hopes for Wainwright.

I started the branch out selling the concept of hot oiling. There was no such thing in the area, and I had to sell the idea that hot oil was the answer for wax control.

This method took time to prove, but prove it we did. It was worth the move. It was also self-satisfying to me. I did not know at this time, it would be the move that paved the way for the future.

# Chapter 40

## Until Death Do We Part

Carl Wood was forty-seven years old and had a bit of a weight problem. Smoking and drinking didn't help. Carl recognized this and decided to slow down. He achieved this by buying a house in Kelowna, British Columbia. He turned over the operation of the forty-five oil wells to his son, as with the half section of his land and house. The hotel in Kerrobert (Saskatchewan?) was turned over to his daughter and son-in-law, and Ronwood was being looked after by Sharon and me.

This was great for Carl and Beth, his wife.

Carl would commute to Calgary biweekly on a cut-rate deal the airline had at the time.

I'd never seen Carl so happy.

One of these trips back to Alberta included a checkup at the doctor's. After the doctor's appointment, Carl came to our house.

We had a business meeting to go over the books and discuss plans for the future. Carl explained what had taken place at the doctor's office. He had gone through tests—blood, treadmill, weight, and generally everything pertaining to his state of physical health. He was ecstatic about all of the tests. He looked great, and I was happy for him.

He left our place and went to his farm that his son was living in.

His daughter-in-law said, "Carl, do you want a cup of tea?"

"Sure," Carl said.

She turned to make tea and heard a loud thump.

This thump was Carl's head hitting the table. Paramedics were summoned, but to no avail. Carl was dead when his head hit the table. He had a massive heart attack, and his life was over.

This was three hours after he left our place.

His daughter called to tell us. I couldn't believe it. I had never dealt with anything like this before.

Carl had been insistent that we have insurance on each other. This we had, and I couldn't think of anything else but Carl's stubbornness about insurance. I wondered if he may have known how things were going to be.

The Wood family was devastated. Everything had happened so unexpectedly.

We at Ronwood were all saddened and confused.

This event was not even contemplated. Although Carl did not have day-to-day control of the company, everyone respected and admired him for his success and business sense.

The funeral came and went as funerals do. Carl was well known in the community, and people showed their love and respect for him.

I was the pallbearer and was proud of performing the task.

After the funeral, as Carl requested, we had an evaluation of the company (Ronwood) and the insurance money that was in effect, paid out Carl's wife, Beth, and the shares transferred to Sharon and me.

Everything went smoothly thanks to our lawyer, Steve Stiles, who had set up Ronwood in the first place.

Our only wrinkle was an overambitious banker who had taken the place of our original banker, Tom Svienson.

This banker said that all the insurance money would have to be put into Ronwood. I said that Carl Wood had died, not Ronwood. Our company was doing just fine with or without Carl.

"Oh well," he said, "that's the way it is."

I went to Steve Stiles and explained what was happening. He said, "Have them get all the papers you have ever signed at the Bank of Montreal, and I'll be there at 10:00 a.m."

I went back to the bank, and they said, "Well, we don't think that's possible."

I replied, "Whatever, Steve will be here at 10:00 a.m. tomorrow."

The next day everything was ready, and I closed out all the accounts.

After the closing of accounts at the Bank of Montreal, the scramble was on to find a bank.

Olds was the logical location for our bank. I went to the Toronto-Dominion Bank and the Alberta Treasury Branch.

I liked the proposal the Treasury Branch made, so that was our new banking institution. They were fantastic. They set up a one-million-dollar debenture system for an operating loan and, of course, a business account.

The manager was great, and we were happy.

# CHAPTER 41

## A Well-Deserved Holiday

After all the events that had transpired, Sharon and I figured a holiday was in order.

Everyone who knew us kept on telling us to take a break and get away for a while.

It was true that we needed a break, but I didn't trust anyone to look after Ronwood.

We had decided, however, to take a five-week tour of London and seven countries in Europe.

This trip started in June of 1983 from Saskatoon, Saskatchewan.

Tim, Jeremy, and Jennifer were no problem. We had Bill and Jean, the anxious Lestock grandparents, to look after them. The kids were as excited to stay with Grandpa and Grandma.

That part was easy as we knew the kids were in good hands.

The next step was boarding the 707 transatlantic jet plane nonstop to London, England. Wow—seven hours flying without a cigarette.

The flight was uneventful, and time passed quickly.

Heathrow Airport was a surprise. I had flown in planes many times before but had never experienced this big of an airport.

Sharon was a great traveler. She observed the signs and directions and led me where I was supposed to be.

The intense scrutiny for weapons, bombs, and hijackers were not as prevalent at that time. Passports were the key to traveling, and we had those documents in order.

We deplaned, picked up our luggage, and pulled them on wheels through Heathrow Airport.

One local bum sitting on a bench smartly yelled out, "BARK BARK!"

This caused the hair on my neck to stand up, and I was ready to fight, except I was well aware that I was in a foreign land. My better judgment let it go. After all, we were supposed to be enjoying ourselves, having fun on holidays.

Off we went to our hotel in the middle of London.

It was beautiful, and we were treated like royalty.

From this hotel we were within walking distance from places such as Hyde Park, Trafalgar Square, Buckingham Palace, and the Tower of London.

We chose, however, to take taxis. I love the taxis of London because they are dangerous. They can maneuver an opening like a race car driver.

Furthermore, they spoke English; and if we wanted to see something special, they would turn the meter off, and we would pay them on the side.

I loved these taxi drivers at that time.

Our next excursion was by Brit Rail to Scotland. The train is the main source of transportation for people travelling along the Coast of England. We were not disappointed and the trip was well worth the time and money.

The people we met along the way were fantastic and very helpful to us. Being Canadian helped because everyone we talked to knew someone in Canada or had relatives living in Canada. There was a lot of Anti Americanism at that time and we spoke like Americans so we had to explain that we were from Western Canada. Perhaps we should have had the Canadian flag sewn on our luggage and coats. I didn't quite understand this dislike for Americans and I always stated that Americans were Canada's best friends and neighbours. This always ended any further conversation about Americans.

Scotland was as I had expected being of Scottish ancestry and the name McGregor made me feel at home.

We stayed at a bed and breakfast home where we were treated like family.

The following morning we rented a car and began to drive along the River Dee.

The trip gave us the true insight into Scotland. The rolling hills, the green grass, the thousands of sheep and the quietness.

I imagined the hills full of men fighting for independence from the King of England and wondered about Rob Roy MacGregor and how related I was to him.

We only spent two days in Scotland and left for London from Aberdeen as our bus tour was scheduled to leave for Europe.

We were exited to leave and boarded the bus for the England Channel at Dover.

There we boarded a hovercraft for France.

After we crossed the channel we boarded our tour bus. We were greeted by our tour guide and bus driver. There were 32 of us on board the tour bus. There were people from many different places and the next four weeks would sort out where they were from and in time there were those who would be friends and those who would not.

Most of the people on the bus were American. As with Canadians, the people from the East were not as friendly and in fact were rude. The Western Americans were friendly and willing to have fun.

The exception to this was a couple from Detroit had their two daughters travelling with them. They were very well travelled, well educated and helpful to us inexperienced travellers. We had a lot of fun with these people from Detroit.

A restaurateur and his wife and father and mother were also on board. At first they were lots of fun and the restaurant owner from New York named Tom was all knowing about Canada, the West, the politics and hockey. He knew it all and wasn't hesitant in letting us know.

As time went on the deficiencies shone through, Tom became wearing on the nerves. He was dominating to the other travellers and his more than 300 lbs. helped to put fear into anyone's mind. No one spoke up or argued with him. No one except me. By the end of our tour we were not friends. We were quite the opposite.

Our trip was full of history, art, religion and wars past. The countries we were privileged to visit were France, Germany, Lichtenstein, Switzerland, Holland, Italy and Spain.

In Italy I was somehow able to contract the infamous dysentery I had diarrhea to the extent that I lost 15 lbs in 10 days. I was determined to fly home on my own at one point. The bus had no bathroom and only at predetermined stops was I able to relieve myself. One of these days was 22 times. I could have written a book on toilet facilities in Europe.

Finally this ailment solved itself in Paris, France.

We finished our tour and continued on to London. We boarded our plane back to Canada and I was never so happy to see Canada again. The contrast between Canada and Europe is like night and day for me. The newness of the building in Canada was most striking. This makes me wonder what it must have been like for the immigrants of the early years. The excitement for them must have been exhilarating. I know that my wife Sharon felt the same. Had I not contracted dysentery, the trip would have been much better because I was not a good companion for her. However she enjoyed the trip and I'm sure she has more good memories than bad.

We arrived in Saskatoon where we began our trip and drove to Lestock to Sharon's parents. Our kids were excited to see us after 5 weeks apart.

I was very happy to be back and I was very anxious to get back to Olds to work again.

After telling all our stories about Europe and England and handing out souvenirs we had bought for everyone we packed up and left for home.

# CHAPTER 42

## Beautiful British Columbia Beckons Once Again

After coming home from our trip overseas, things weren't the same without Carl Wood. My motivation to expand further was not as it was when Carl was alive. Working every day and into the night left little time for fun and family. I felt I was missing out on life.

The answer I felt was to sell out. Sharon agreed and we put Ronwood up for sale.

This was no easy task we were to find out soon. The business was specialized and there weren't many buyers with the experience needed to run a hot oil, pressure truck and steam cleaning business. The profit ability was good but not high enough to attract an investor.

We kept trying to sell and went through several propositions but none developed to finality.

One day in the winter of 1984 a man by the name of Wayne Cruikshank approached us about the sale of Ronwood.

We had done a lot of work for his dad: Jack Cruikshank and Jack was a superintendent for Shell Oil at that time.

We sat down and discussed our operation and I was willing to train Wayne for running the operation.

An offer was made but he wanted no part of Wainwright where Joe Rinas was settled running the one truck operation.

Wayne felt it was too far away to look after. I decided to keep the Wainwright part of Ronwood and changed the name to Alberta Hot Oil Services Ltd. I also started the sale of the one truck operation and the acreage I had bought to rent Joe and his wife Darlene.

Everything fell into place and we had a selling out party to introduce Wayne to the customers we had. The party was well attended at the Legion hall of Olds. There were around 200 people and Wayne got introduced to everyone as the new owner of Ronwood.

Wayne was brought up in the Olds so he already knew a good portion of the crowd. He mixed well and this seemed to be a good move for him.

There were some hurdles to jump over. I had sold one of the hot oilers to Jim Knapp and my brother Orville also was a contract operator with the steam truck and pressure washing operation.

Neither Orville or Jim stayed with Wayne as they had with me. This immediately created competition for Wayne. He was in for a rough ride.

Once the sale of Ronwood Petroleum Services Ltd was finalized I immediately registered the business name of Ronwood Enterprises Ltd. Somehow I must have known that I would be back in Alberta and I would reactivate the Ronwood name once again.

This was not in my plans at the beginning but as things were to turn out years later this proved to be a very smart move.

We put our four level split home up for sale and started planning for the move to Kelowna, B.C.

Our house sold and our moving date coincided with the finish of the school year for our kids.

We purchased a house in Kelowna to move into.

We also want to North Battleford Saskatchewan and purchased a boat. A 16.5 ft with an inboard motor. We felt that a boat was an absolute necessity because of all the lakes within close proximity to Kelowna. The infamous Lake Okanagan with the legendary Ogopogo sea serpent was the largest lake that Kelowna was built around. There were many Marinas and boat launches to accommodate such a boat.

We were exited to start out this new part of our lives.

The house we bought on Glenmore Drive had two levels of 2400 sq. ft. The house was finished with a swimming pool in the back yard and a pool table in the rumpus room.

I installed a pool heater to keep the water a consistent temperature and an underground irrigation system for watering the shrubs, plants and grass surrounding the house.

My best friend Jack O'Connor was well situated in Kelowna and he was a fountain of information for us. He and his wife Doreen had two children. One boy and one girl.

They were around the same age as our three so their lives became friendships forever.

School was close by and went as far as grade eight. After grade eight the progression was to go to Kelowna Senior Secondary or KSS as the school was called.

Tim, Jeremy and Jennifer were all athletic and Kelowna had all the sports to get involved with.

Being familiar with hockey and baseball, Tim and Jeremy both excelled in these two sports. Jennifer was an excellent swimmer and was into piano. She also joined the ringette team for girls.

Everyone was occupied

I purchased a steam cleaning/pressure washing business. I rented a bay in a shop complex that was reasonably close to our house

Some business came with the truck so I started working immediately cleaning heavy equipment, logging trucks, mining equipment and various small cleaning jobs kept me busy to start.

This wasn't enough for me however. I decided to build another steam truck and pick up more work. I brought one of my drivers from Olds over to operate. This was Byron Laviolette. He was ready for a change and came to Kelowna in a hurry. He was single and adventurous. He moved in with us and was like a member of our family. We worked well together and searched out more work for the two trucks. This was all good except the competition was such that the rate per hour was cut down too much to make a decent profit.

I had enough free time to get heavily involved with baseball as President of Kelowna Minor Baseball. This took much of my time in the summer. In the winter I coached hockey. Both sports demanded a lot of my time but I loved it. My buddy Jack was heavy into hockey. Between us, we put many many volunteer hours into the two sports. Coaching, umpiring, executive duties, practices, games against teams throughout B.C and Alberta. We did a lot of travelling and organizing to keep our kids involved in as high of a calibre of sport that was offered.

This kept us all busy.

Baseball was the biggest time consumer for me as being President meant fundraising, scheduling for 80 teams, equipment purchasing and of course dealing with parent problems. When Sharon and I first got involved, Kelowna Minor Baseball was almost without funds to operate.

We met Bob Stewart who was intent on turning this around. He was instrumental in getting me to take on the President's job.

At this time a Bingo Hall was opened in Kelowna.

In order for this Bingo Hall to operate they needed only non profit organization, such as Kelowna Minor Baseball to sponsor bingo nights. The

Bingo Hall would take part of the profit leaving the rest to the non profit organizations.

We had to provide workers of course. This took more organizing but the profits were very good.

Within months we had a surplus of money to provide equipment for most of the teams in baseball. With donations from local business proceeds from 2 concession stands and the bingo money we were soon in great shape financially

We shaped up seven ball diamonds, rebuilt the two concession stands and made our teams highly competitive. We were proud to be involved

We were in a position to host provincial playoffs and even one Western Canadian Championships

This was accomplished with the good fortune of money from the bingos and many volunteers.

At this time a friend from Olds by the name of Russ Sych liked travelling over to Kelowna and we got involved in some property. One was a lot on the west side of Lake Okanagan purely speculative.

The other property was 2½ acres of commercial land with a large building that had been used for manufacturing windows and doors. The business that was operating out of this building went into bankruptcy.

We purchased this property at a low price.

There was a residence on one end of the large building that was very livable.

Byron, my employee moved out of our house and lived there. We let the rental bay go in Kelowna where we were paying rent and parked in the building Russ and I had purchased.

I sold one of the steamer trucks and sold the other to Byron on a percentage basis.

This freed me from the business but financially I was hurting.

# CHAPTER 43

# He ain't heavy,
# He's my brother

Around this time, my brother Malcolm and his wife Rosalie were involved in a riding stable and a soup and sandwich restaurant in Kelowna.

The debt load was too much and they approached Sharon and myself to buy into the restaurant

We did this to help out but the profit was low. Sharon worked at the restaurant which was called The LITTLE HOBO in the middle of downtown Kelowna.

The location was great but there were several other similar operations competing for the same clientele. The morning coffee, lunch and afternoon coffee crowd was the extent of business. This wasn't nearly enough to support two households. Eventually I would buy Malcolm and Rosalie out completely. Even then the business was not profitable enough.

Between the restaurant, the steam truck and the property investment there wasn't enough money left over to carry our living expenses. We were going downhill fast financially.

We put our beautiful house with the swimming pool up for sale and purchased a lower priced home. I sold our boat and we cut expenses.

A good friend I made through baseball named Ron Reiter was a purchase agent for the city of Kelowna. At this time the City of Kelowna was building a water treatment/sewage plant. Ron let me know that they would need an operator when they finished. This seemed to be a good opportunity except for the union would also be involved. I hated unions but the wages would be good.

During this time I made a phone call to Joe Rinas in Wainwright, Alberta. Joe is who I sold the hot oil truck and the business of Alberta Hot Oil Services to along with the sale was a 1970 Chev pick up.

I phoned to see if I could buy this truck to fix up for the boys as Tim was getting to the driving age. As it turned out, the truck was too beat up and rusted to restore.

However out of this phone call came another work opportunity. Joe had just purchased another hot oil truck from Wayne Cruikshank who I had sold out to in Olds. Joe had the truck but no operator. I said I would come and run it if I could purchase it. This meant that Joe would carry the down payment to secure financing and I would pay a 17% percentage of gross income from the truck. The location would be Consort, Alberta.

The wheels began to turn and decisions were made that would change the course of our lives forever.

# Chapter 44

# Alberta Bound

This was not a hard decision to make but we weren't sure about the little place called CONSORT. I had worked a little there doing some sporatic hot oil work but I knew very little about the community.

We did some checking through the local newspaper in Consort, some real estate inquiries, school and hospital facilities and what the people were like in the area. Everything checked out on the positive side.

We drove to Consort to find something to live in which turned out to be one above average house for sale.

We sold our house in Kelowna and put a down payment on the house in Consort. I sold everything I had an interest in by this time in Kelowna. The steam truck, the property and the restaurant. We didn't have much cash left but our credit was good and we had enough to start over in the oil patch again.

This was June of 1989 and the school year was ending. We organized everything so that Tim, Jeremy and Jennifer would have the summer to familiarize themselves with their new surroundings. This proved valuable upon starting into a new school

Jennifer had the hardest time moving into Consort. She would have started high school at KSS in Kelowna with her friends but that all changed with the move to Consort. We tried to make the change as comfortable as possible but the change was within herself. She made every effort to make the change in her life work but I am sure that she always blamed me for failing to make things work in Kelowna which would have allowed her to finish her education in British Columbia with her friends. She and I had many fights during her teenage years and one of these fights ended in her leaving home but only a short time elapsed before she came back.

I hurt terribly inside but I would not relent to ask her to come home. For that I wonder if she ever thought I didn't love her enough. That I know wasn't true and later on I am sure I proved I would die for her. This time would not be the only time we turned against one another. More serious times lie ahead.

The boys were happy to be in Consort. They were included in sports, school and became well respected in the community.

They had their conflicts establishing their place but in all actuality these conflicts were small encumbrance

Our lives in Consort were busy as they were in Kelowna. Immediately I got involved with sports, met the locals and of course was involved in the oil patch with my hot oil truck.

The oil patch was extremely busy around Consort as they had discovered a new zone called the Dina Zone. This was a lucrative discovery and yielded a high wax content which made my type of work invaluable. By knowing what to do about this wax problem in the wells and the pipelines helped me out immensely in the specialized business of hot oiling.

As with any new venture in a new area the business did not happen overnight. Patience and persistence were always the key factors. When jobs came up I did the job right and word got around.

The Consort area was very active. This was due to the Dina discovery and the old wells were called Viking wells. Both zones were waxy. The perfect situation for hot oiling. There were many chemical companies in this area claiming to have the chemical to solve the wax problem. This was costly but the hot oil method always fought the chemical method. I was never adverse to chemical but I always proclaimed chemical will not work without heat. I was right but I didn't have the resources that the chemical companies had at their disposal to push their system.

This push was usually done in the head offices in Calgary.

The local operators of the oil wells called battery operators knew my system was better but they only answered to their bosses in Calgary.

My objective was simple. All I had to do was keep one truck busy enough to make payments to the Royal Bank of Canada. Expenses incurred from the operation plus our living expenses had to be covered.

Due to the arrangement with Joe Rinas and Alberta Hot oil, 17% of total revenue also had to be paid.

We struggled but we made all of our commitments.

Alberta Hot Oil was not as busy at Wainwright. I did my best to give them any overflow work that I had at Consort. I felt I was being generous to give them this work.

However, two incidents occurred to change everything.

My son Tim was licensed to drive and I was using him as a spare driver to relieve me during long hour jobs.

Joe took exception to this and said that Tim was too young to do the job by himself. This statement made me angry

Tim was an exceptional operator. He trained easily and was very conscientious about his duties. I had trained many operators in the past and I knew where to leave someone on their own, without on site supervision.

Tim was one of these types. Not only had I trained him, he also spent many hours with me as a boy because he loved it.

I knew this but Joe was afraid something bad would happen that Tim couldn't handle and this would come back on Alberta Hot oil costing Joe money.

This I could understand but I thought he was being unreasonable.

I backed off and I quit leaving Tim on his own.

The next situation came up when Joe approached me for more work in the Consort area.

This involved work that I was already giving to them.

Joe sat in my hot oiler one day and said "We need more work for our trucks."

"Fine" I said.

"Weekday work." Joe said.

I got very angry at this and said "That isn't going to happen, Joe. If I'm going to work all the weekends and holidays and your trucks are going to work weekdays you can fuck yourself. Don't forget who started you out and put you into Wainwright in the first place."

"And how many times will I have to hear that same old song?" Joe said.

"Never again Joe. Get out of my truck."

I was mad and he knew it. He left and I pondered my situation.

Joe was carrying $36,000.00 down payment money on my truck and I had no idea how to pay him releasing me from this debt. The ace I held in my hand was Joe's neglect of the terms of our operating contract between our two companies. This contract was to be annually renewed, changing the terms if necessary and dated and signed.

This was not kept up thereby negating the operating agreement.

I knew this and approached my banker to discuss the situation. The bank held the balance of the loan on the truck as well as an operating loan on my receivables from Alberta Hot Oil.

The banker, Jack Reynolds immediately agreed to pay out Alberta Hot Oil and between what was owing to Ronwood and the bank taking over receivables from Alberta Hot Oil I was able to start as Ronwood on its own set of books.

This gave Ronwood 17% more income to cover extra expenses.

I was flying on my own power again. This was a great feeling and I was up for the challenge of competing against Alberta Hot oil even though I only had one truck. There were many oil companies glad to know they were dealing with the owner on every job. I also had plenty of experience to work with.

Another advantage I had was a tank truck company based out of Consort that was more than willing to help out as far as turning work my way as they didn't have any hot oilers or pressure trucks. This was left to my devices.

This should have stacked the cards in my favour.

There were jokers in the deck of cards. These were going to be most troublesome for me.

# CHAPTER 45

## Things I Couldn't Change

One problem that arose from time to time throughout the years in Olds, Kelowna and now Consort was the Manic Depression, or as it is now called Bi Polar.

For this I was being attended to in Kelowna by a psychiatrist and I was on a steady diet of Lithium. I attended AA part time to control the drinking. However my attendance at AA (ALCOHOLIC ANONYMOUS) was just that PART TIME! To be successful in AA you must dedicate full time or it just doesn't work.

This was one joker I wasn't able to deal with and in every geological change I made he was on my shoulder. I never was able to shake this problem. Probably because I didn't want to but whatever the reason this was my nemesis as smart as I thought I was, he was smarter.

I had great help in all three places from AA. People who had been in dire straits with alcohol. People who had fought the fight and understood that the fight was never over.

I couldn't get to this point of surrender. The better I felt after a period of sobriety, the more I thought I could drink under moderation. There was no such thing for me. This I wouldn't accept so I would pay the consequences time after time.

Suspended licenses, accidents, fights, family difficulties, lying, cheating, lack of performance on the job, passing responsibilities over to Sharon my wife and making her make excuses for me were all because I would play the game I couldn't play. Alcohol was burning my soul and I was eventually going to provide the match that would light an uncontrollable flame

As I said there were hands out willing to help in Olds, Kelowna and Consort. Consort was the best group of all and for that I was grateful. There were only about twelve steady members but I felt at home with these people. Some of these were involved in the oil industry so we had two things in common Oil and Alcohol.

Our meetings were on Thursdays every week and I have to admit I always looked for an excuse to miss the meetings.

Sharon was willing to find out more about my problem and joined Alanon for people who weren't alcoholic or had problems with alcohol but these were people who were affected by people with alcohol problems.

Learning to live with alcoholics was the main them of Alanon.

Sharon tried but she had a hard time dealing with a problem that wasn't hers.

I believe she had her hands full of other things like raising a family of three, doing books for the business, answering the phone to book work, dealing with the bank and having a social life with the Lion's Club of Consort. She was strong enough to deal with everything life had to offer at any time but she couldn't deal with what I couldn't deal with.

This problem was more baffling to her than I knew.

# CHAPTER 46

# He Who Has The Gold Rules

After the hot oil truck was 100% owned by Ronwood and the Royal Bank, I discovered quickly that I didn't have enough equipment to do all the work that was coming in.

I approached my banker and the answer was a firm "NO!" He wanted me to go for another year first before incurring any more debt load.

This was good, conservative thinking but the opportunity that was there now wouldn't be there in a year. Furthermore it took months to rig up equipment.

I saw his point and thought of waiting one year.

However, the oil companies kept phoning for trucks that I didn't have I was booked solid for 2 weeks in advance. This was a good thing but I was afraid of losing all of my work if a company decided to move in to Consort.

I decided to try another bank. I travelled to Coronation, 30 miles west to the Alberta Treasury Branch. The manager was more than happy to deal on another truck. This would be a pressure truck. The equipment was the same as a hot oiler without the hot oil burner. This made operating easier and this would take the load of pressure work off the existing hot oiler I was operating. In my mind this was a good plan.

We went through the financing, the rig up and everything was rolling as it should be.

Although this has never been proven this is what I am sure happened to almost break us.

The Royal Bank manager was holding our accounts receivable as security for our operating loan. The hot oil truck still had money owing against it and when he found out we had borrowed to build this pressure truck at the Alberta Treasury Branch he immediately picked up the phone and called me.

It was about 3:30 PM on a week day. I answered and this bank manager said "We are calling your loans."

I said "Pardon me?"

He said "The Royal Bank is requesting payment of your operating loan and the Hot Oil Truck."

I said "You can't do that on the Hot Oil Truck."

He said "Yes we can and in effect Ronwood is finished as of tomorrow."

I simply said "Fuck you!" and hung up the phone.

I knew I was in big trouble with nowhere to turn and I broke down and started crying uncontrollably.

Tim, my son came home from school at this time and saw me. He asked "What's wrong Dad?"

I told Tim and he was upset because this operation was important to him too.

Tim, Jeremy and I had built a 40' x 20' shop for the hot oiler. It was just a stick build shop but it had a cement floor and sewed the purpose at that stage.

We were proud of what we had and we didn't want to lose it all.

I went in to Consort to see my friend the tank truck business owner.

I told him what had happened and he picked up the phone to his finance man in Edmonton who held all the financing on the 10 or 12 tank trucks.

John Laan was the name of the guy in the Edmonton, Alberta. The name of his company was Airways Leasing and Financing. At that time John loved to take on deals like mine and he trusted Gary Stevens completely

There was one catch to this deal. To enable this buyout from the Royal Bank, Sharon and I would have to relinquish 50% of Ronwood to Double S transport that was the name of the tank truck company Gary and Pat Stevens owned.

Sharon and I discussed this but we had nowhere to turn. No one we knew had that kind of money.

We went through with the deal and the Royal Bank was out of Ronwood.

We dealt with the Alberta Treasury Branch only after this.

Gary and I figured that we could expand Ronwood faster this way and Sharon and I would come out further ahead.

Sometimes you need to do these mergers to keep up with the competition. This was the theory and it should have worked.

But the best laid plans of mice and men will often go astray.

# CHAPTER 46B

## Déjà Vu All Over Again

At this point in time I needed good experienced men whom I could trust with the expensive equipment we were buying and rigging up. Times were changing and technology was moving fast.

Keith Beres, Sharon's youngest brother who had worked for me in Crossfield on the maintenance truck and also in Olds as a hot oil operator was in Regina working for IPSCO making pipe.

Things were slow in Regina and Keith was getting anxious about money.

We talked about what I was doing and not wanting to push him too hard I was careful in our conversations not to seem too desperate for men.

Keith was cautious, conservative and he didn't want to get locked into something he couldn't get out of.

He was also loyal to any commitment he made.

We discussed the job, the wage and the living arrangements.

He would be living with Sharon and I to start with and I would train him on a hot oil unit that we had bought from Drayton Valley.

Keith also needed time to visit his wife and two boys who were living in Wilcox Saskatchewan.

This was all fine with us because we knew Keith would do the job and eventually everything would fall into place.

Alliance, Alberta was about 80 miles north west of Consort and Tim our son was living there running a hot oiler. We needed Keith there so we started to slowly put Keith into that area

An acreage which included 14 acres of land, a house and various outbuildings came up for sale just east of Alliance 12 miles.

Keith made an offer which was accepted and this became the home of Keith, Michelle Cody and Bronson.

We had purchased a shop in Alliance but as there was a shop on Keith's acreage we used that for Keith to run his hot oiler out of.

Keith looked after the work around Alliance and Michelle moved from Wilcox to make Alliance her home.

In 1999 Keith and Michelle bought the hot oiler from Ronwood and operated as "Skeeters."

About this time frame another ex employee from Olds entered the scene. Richard Laviolette was eager to get into something long term. With a young wife and a short bank account, Richard was easy to convince that he should come back to work for Ronwood in Consort

Richard could start in anywhere anytime with total confidence in what he was expected to do. He was another hand I could count on.

The third man I was happy to have come on board was Byron Laviolette also from the Olds chapter of Ronwood and working with me in Kelowna. He was exited to work after having had his serious highway traffic accident at Fox Creek Alberta.

These three were instrumental in providing valuable experience to make Ronwood into a company that knew what to do on the job.

This is what I needed at this time and they gave me all they had to give

# CHAPTER 47

# Back To Where The Story All Began

John Laan and Airways Leasing were fantastic to deal with. He was fast, efficient but he was also high priced financing with always a buy out at the end of any agreement.

This is all fine and dandy if things roll right.

But as in any business especially in the Oil Patch there are ups and there are downs.

1995 was one of these downturns. By this time we had 2 hot oilers, one more being built, 2 flush by service rigs, steam truck, one pressure truck.

Most of the equipment was busy but the Consort—Provost area was slowing down. The oil companies around Consort were beginning to drill in South West Saskatchewan.

We were called to travel this six hours to do work there. Some of these trips to the Gull Lake area were hard on equipment and costly for the oil companies to pick up the travel time.

The natural solution to this problem I thought was to move 2 trucks to Gull Lake. One truck would be a hot oiler the other would be the Steam/Pressure truck combination.

We also had 2 small one ton pressure trucks. If the work warranted it, one of those would also be moved to Gull Lake

My hopes were high for this to work most likely because I had been born and raised in Gull Lake and I had something to prove.

The risk was high but I worked hard to make this work out.

My nephew Richard Piechotta who was the son of my eldest sister Lois had inherited our home half section of land with some buildings. One of these buildings was the house that the McGregor family was raised in.

There was no shop to work out of but we rented a bay to keep the steamer in because this had to be protected from freezing.

I bought a field office/trailer and a camping style trailer to live in.

I bought tanks, a backhoe, and dug holes to set the tanks into on their sides.

We then proceeded to take oil, dirt, sand and drilling mud to put into one tank, super heat the mixture and take the oil and sell it.

We made a deal with the Municipality of Webb to take the dirt, sand and cement to spread on their roads.

This was a heavy work load for me especially.

I lived, ate and slept work to make this a success.

The oil companies around Gull Lake were under pressure to clean up the open pits in the area of which there were many.

The solids from the oil had to be removed to enable shipping clean oil through their tanks and pipelines. Heat and chemical would usually separate the oil and dirt but sometimes this didn't happen easily.

I was stubborn and money was no object. This proved costly and the trucks that were supposed to be busy weren't.

Things were starting to go downhill fast. I saw this but I wasn't giving up.

Bob Davies was one of my employees in Consort working out of Alliance. I had hired him away from Alberta Hot oil because Joe Rinas and Bob did not get along. I had sent Bob to Joe to work and was sorry things did not work out.

I knew Bob was a good hand. So I wasn't afraid to hire him. He was running a hot oiler for me in Alliance when I moved equipment to Gull Lake. I decided to move Bob and his family to Gull Lake to help me.

We were buying solvent, inhibitor and dispersants from a chemical company at this time and they made the suggestion that we should split Bob's monthly income and they would use him as a salesman. Bob was great at that and the big advantage was he also was born and raised in Gull Lake.

This should have all fallen into place.

After a few months, the Solvent company decided they wanted Bob to work 100% for them.

Not wanting to stand in the way I agreed and Bob no longer worked for me.

This proved to be the wrong move because they dealt Bob a bad hand and let him go the day after Bob's mother's funeral.

At this point I didn't have enough work to rehire him and I was ready to pull out of Gull Lake.

As in many times in my past I let the pressure get to me and turned to drinking thinking that would solve everything.

At this point I had hired two teenage girls to run trucks.

One of these girls was Bob's daughter. Had there been enough work everything would have worked out but this was not happening.

I let Kim/Bob's daughter go and kept the other girl on. She was trained better to handle the steamer and pressure work. She, too was determined to make things work for Ronwood. As try as we might there was not enough work at that time and I had to finally admit it.

I tried to undo the drinking I had started by going to Alcoholics Anonymous in Gull Lake and Swift Current.

This only ended up to be a farce. I was only pretending and my intentions were far from sincere.

All of this ended up in affairs with three women, more drinking and an accident which resulted in a loss of my driver's license

All of this commotion was not going unnoticed by Sharon who was running Ronwood in Consort.

She was dealing with the busy end and paying the bills so she knew this was not viable in Gull Lake and she definitely knew there was more going on than just work.

# CHAPTER 48

## Survival By Elimination

During this period I had rehired Byron Laviolette who had previously worked for me in Olds, Kelowna and now Consort.

Byron had a very bad car accident in North Western Alberta which left him in bad shape. He spent a long time recovering in hospitals and there was a law suit which he won and was awarded money.

When he received the money I had hired him to work for Ronwood in Consort.

At this time we were selling investment bundles where we would pay a high return on investments of money to boost the value of Ronwood and allow us to expand.

Byron thought this was a good deal for him so he invested around $75,000.00.

I set Byron up as manager while I was in Gull Lake to help Sharon manage.

We also had a good looking blond secretary/receptionist that Byron became more than interested in. This was fine at first but then I think that Byron's position and investment went to his head and he became really pushy with Sharon.

One day he told her where to go and Sharon phoned me. I rushed to Consort from Gull Lake and fired both Byron and the secretary.

Byron thought he had the upper hand with his investment but I had a 90 day pay out clause built in so I made him wait the full ninety days. This credited a life long division between Byron and myself. Neither one of us came out on top but the taste lingered sour.

These investment bundles were held by Sharon's father Bill Beres followed by his second wife Helen Vass. The others were Helen's son and daughter in law. These amounts totalled around $500,000.

Another $50,000 was borrowed from Sharon's dad Bill on a razor sharpening invention by our 50% partner in Ronwood. This deal was done between the two outside of our company.

As time went on, business slowed and things were manageable but rough waters were ahead.

One great evening the phone rang and it was John Laan our finance man from Edmonton

He explained clearly what he required from Sharon and myself. This was a complete refinancing of all the equipment he had on lien.

I vehemently disputed this with him. He explained that Gary Stevens had borrowed money with his brother on Cats and tanks that wasn't able to be repaid along with his collateral was his 50% of Ronwood. I knew nothing about this deal.

John said that he would be sending drivers from Edmonton

I said that he didn't have to do that and that I had drivers to take the trucks to Edmonton. In fact I would even drive one myself and I hung up the phone.

One half hour later John phoned back and offered another payout figure. We would continue on paying as we had been with an extra buyout price on the end. Sharon and I agreed to these terms only if Gary Stevens was left out of all the paperwork. This was agreed upon and Gary Stevens was left out of Ronwood.

A phone call came later from Gary calling me names that are not on my birth certificate but we saved our company.

The money owing to investors and our accounts payable remained the same. The money owed Sharon's Dad Bill was to be paid by Gary. I knew that would never happen and I was right.

# CHAPTER 49

## Payback Time

This was the most serious situation we had ever been in because there were investors to pay back. As well, these investors were family. There's nothing worse than family when money is involved.

They were more than patient and as long as the interest we promised was paid they could and would all wait for the principal.

We started selling off equipment that wasn't paying back.

We sold the flush by trucks which were a heavy burden and required more men to operate.

We sold the steamer/pressure truck the two small pressure trucks and the two biggest hot oilers.

We kept one hot oiler, sub contracted the newest hot oiler from the man who bought it for a percentage of the income.

Eventually we were seeing daylight again.

Keith and Michelle who were now permanently settled in Alliance on the acreage they bought decided to purchase the hot oil truck he was operating for me. This was good for both Ronwood and for them. Keith was careful with money and I had no fear he would do well on his own. Michelle was good with people and they soon got to be popular in the area. Another good thing was that Michelle and I got along very well. This sometimes doesn't happen with spouses in business.

Our good relationship is still intact through a lot of bad times

I gave Keith all the help I could and I was happy to be able to provide the help

During this time of repayment and restructuring I was working too many hours again such as was the case in Gull Lake.

I had a good idea as to how to build a small one ton truck with small pumping equipment under a topper flush with the box. It worked perfectly and was quite a hit with our customers. I built a steamer in a trailer to pull behind so I could do many jobs with this combination.

One day while I was repairing a barb wire fence at our acreage my cell phone rang and it was Krista my daughter in law, Jeremy's wife. She was expressing her feelings over how I favored Tim over Jeremy and that Jeremy got all the shit equipment to run. On and on it went until I just hung up and threw down what I had in my hands and said fuck it all.

I jumped into this one ton truck and took off out of the yard. Directly to the Consort Bar.

It wasn't hard to find someone to drink with in Consort especially at that time of day. It was 5:00 o'clock and work was over for most people.

I probably had 6 drinks by seven o'clock and picked up a case of beer for the road. Had I have stopped at home I would have been okay but I knew Sharon would be mad as hell because she knew I was in the bar by then.

I carried on south and east with one destination in mind—GULL LAKE, SASKATCHEWAN.

My mind always seemed to turn to Gull Lake in times like these. Why still remains a mystery but more times than not Gull Lake spelled trouble for me.

Sharon hated the place and she had many reasons to.

I was on my way and I had that don't give a shit attitude that always led to big problems.

I ended up driving on the Trans Canada Highway which at that time was still two laned

There was a line of traffic ahead but I guess I figured I could pass safely. I guessed wrong and hit a car head on causing the car to barrel roll into the car behind me. A girl was driving the car I hit and her boyfriend was sleeping in the back with a dog. He was killed as well as the dog.

There was mayhem on the highway. It was very fortunate only one was killed. For that I am very sorry and think of this mistake daily.

There were the usual emergency people out and I was eventually taken to the MAPLE Creek Police Station where I was tested for alcohol blood level.

I was put in the lock up until a judge was available to set bail. I was released on bail and went home feeling as sorry for myself as I had ever felt. Sharon came to Maple Creek to pick me up and there wasn't too much to be said. We were both concerned about what may happen next. I knew I would face jail time but I didn't know how much time. These were the darkest of days for me.

I was 53 years old and I should well have known better.

I had a great wife, a business that was just coming around to the block again, three wonderful children of which two were married with children which made me a grandparent.

This had to stop and this was enough of a shock to me as anyone. Would the drinking problems ever stop?

# CHAPTER 50

## JAIL!!
## (A Small Price To Pay)

After the accident, the truck I was driving was a write off. I replaced it with a new truck and switched the equipment in the box over to the new one. This was no big deal.

The big deal was facing charges for what had happened.

I was charged with multiple charges of dangerous driving, driving over .08, and passing while unsafe to do so. There were all condensed to Dangerous Driving causing death. This one charge carried a maximum sentence of 14 years in jail.

I hired one of the top lawyers in Saskatchewan and he was high priced. By the time everything was through the price was $40,000.00.

This was a small price to pay as the insurance company carrying our insurance paid out over one million in damages and settlements

I repaid a very small percentage in increased premiums.

The sentencing was carried out in January, 2000 and the sentence was 15 months in the Regina Correction Center which was a provincial jail. I would receive time off for good behaviour and could be out of jail in only six months.

This was reason to celebrate I suppose but I was terribly fearful of jail. I had never spent serious time except for the time I spent in B.C. That was in a forestry camp. This jail was for real.

I didn't get any time to contemplate my situation. I was put into the Swift Current lock up cell for a night and a day. I was then transported to Regina by a police van.

From the van to the check in at the correctional center was the longest walk I can ever remember taking.

There is no politeness, no compassion and the guards could care less about who you are or where you came from.

The guards had their job to do and I can imagine that they deal with some real assholes every day. This I can confirm now from experience in this environment.

I was checked into the oldest part of the correctional center.

The walls were carved with names of the past falling away with the plaster and paint long overdue to be replaced.

Louis Riel had stayed in these cells in the 1800's awaiting trial to be hung for treason against the Canadian Government

I was a part of history I thought but that didn't help. I wasn't in for idealism. I was in here for stupidity.

The time ahead is long when you count down the days. I learned to not count.

I waited in the old cells sharing a cell with three others. There was not much to learn from them. They were revolving prisoners and this wasn't their first rodeo.

There are some who commit crimes during the winter months to be able to have three meals and a warm bed for the cold months in Canada.

About one week went by before I was transferred to a newer cell block.

These cell blocks had individual units where each prisoner had a bed, a TV, a toilet and sink in a 9'x6' room.

This doesn't seem like much but this is far superior to doing time with 3 others in a small space.

The first meal I experienced was supper. The cells all opened onto a common eating area with tables and chairs. Most prisoners had their spot to sit unless an argument or fight ensued then they would usually relocate.

I came out of my cell for the first meal not knowing anything about where I was supposed to eat or where to sit. I was standing outside my cell door with fear and confusion written all over my face when a chair came sliding across the floor towards me.

A large man around the 300 pound mark with long red hair and a beard loudly proclaimed "White men sit here" I looked around and every eye was fixed on me

I obediently grabbed the chair and pulled it up to the table he was sitting at.

It didn't take long to figure out who was in control of all of them. They had fear of him and respect for him.

His name was Clayton but everyone called him 'RED'.

As it turned out he was from Swift Current and we had some common acquaintances. This was right on and we were friends for all my jail time.

Two years less a day which was the maximum sentence in a minimum security correctional centre.

Everyone who wanted to work could apply for jobs within the prison system. Red chose woodworking and I chose maintenance and repair.

Smoking was not allowed in Regina but there were ways to get tobacco or various other substances that weren't allowed.

This was done by trade. You would place an order for canteen then trade those away for tobacco or whatever was smuggled in.

Red was a master of getting tobacco, lighters, cigarettes and occasionally alcohol.

He was careful and selective. He was not going to get caught because this meant more time and he was not about to get shafted by the dead heads that couldn't pay for what he smuggled. No one could play the game as well as Rod could.

I was a heavy smoker when I came in and this no smoking rule was hard to put up with.

Another means of getting some smoking material was my cousin Dave who was a long time guard in this jail. He had to be very cautious because of his job and I had to be careful not to get too close to any guard for fear of reprisal from the other inmate.

We rolled tobacco into the pages from the Bible then used tin foil to create a spark from a wall plug in to light a kleenex on fire creativity at its best. It is simply amazing how powerful an addiction can be. Smoking is the most powerful of all.

The guards would sometimes raid our cells to find any smoking materials but mostly they ignored the problem.

Their jobs were much easier when they got along with the prisoners as the prisoners were an angle in JAIL.

The days went by painfully slow. Knowing you couldn't walk out the door and go home made minutes into hours and hours into days.

Although I was working some of the time there were many days such as weekends and holidays when we didn't work. Those days were the longest. Thank God for Television being allowed.

I read a lot from the library resources such as they were and I wrote letters. The more I wrote the more I would get back. The phone was available but only at certain times.

My favorite escape from the locked up atmosphere were the Alcoholics Anonymous meetings.

These meetings were the same as anywhere. The stories were similar and the reason we were here was because of drugs or alcohol or both.

Church on Sunday was another way to pass some time. This didn't do any harm but I never met anyone who turned religious because of jail church.

Most of my time was spent in my little cell. TV was my companion and reflecting on the mistakes and bad choices I had made to get here took the rest of my waking hours.

Four months of locked up time was what I put in.

After four months I was eligible to apply to be in a half way house. This was what everyone wanted because there was more freedom. The food was better, you could smoke and you could work if there was work available.

The application was complex but the complexity was worth the reward.

# CHAPTER 51

## Vacation TIME!

During this transition time between the Regina Correctional Center and the Halfway house, the jail warden received a phone call from a crown prosecutor from Lethbridge Alberta advising him that I was to appear in Court in Alberta. This message was relayed to me and I was in shock.

I had no other charges to face and this would definitely affect my release from jail.

Finally after a few days of agony over not knowing what that was about, I was allowed to talk to the crown prosecutor. She explained that this was not a charge against me but that I was a key witness to an accident on a job where I was working.

The company charged was Terreco Industries and they faced five charges of which were serious.

No one was killed or seriously injured but this was more luck than good planning on Terreco's part.

I advised her (crown prosecutor) of where I was and asked if the time could be delayed until I was back in Alberta.

She advised me that this was not feasible and that they had made plans to get me to court to testify.

When I hung up the phone I wasn't too concerned until I talked to the guard who had my travel plan in hand

I figured a plane or a police car but I was so wrong.

My trip was inclusive of handcuffs, leg irons and traveled in a paddy wagon with stopover at every jail along the longest route you could take to Coronation, Alberta. This was only thirty miles from my home town of Consort.

Aside from the Police Station lock ups were Edmonton Remand and Red Deer Remand Centers.

These remands were a mix of hardened long time prisoners along with short timers such as myself

I witnessed one beating of which I claimed I didn't see and I met some very interesting cell mates who shared their hard time stories and the two weeks were more interesting than the many boring nights in Regina.

This time cut my time short when I returned and I was glad for that.

I spent many hours finishing my sentence at the half way house attending AA meetings in Regina's many meeting places

I was never so happy to be an AA member as then.

At one of these times, there was an AA seminar.

I attended this and I was shocked to see three of my friends from AA in Consort.

They were there for three days and this was a bonus for me. The world can be small at times.

Soon after my tour back to Alberta and some more time in the half way house I was released on probation. My probation officers were the RCMP in Consort and another in Stettler, Alberta. My driver's license was suspended for five years.

I adhered to these terms very carefully because I didn't want to end up back in jail and being caught driving meant more time without a license.

My wife Sharon sacrificed a lot for me at this time. She drove me everywhere I had to be. I was not the best person to have beside her most of the time and the road condition were not good most of the time.

The winter months were dangerous as one time a semi pulled out in front of us in a foggy morning going to a job. She turned into the ditch to avoid a collision and crossed two other ditches before coming to a stop wrapped in barbed wire. She did it all right.

There were severely cold days, long hours, severely hot days in the summer but she persevered the five years better than I did.

# CHAPTER 52

## The Road to Recovery

I knew that the way to get out of this mess was to work hard, keep the debt load down and stay away from the booze.

Alcoholics Anonymous played a big part at this point in time.

My friends in the Consort AA group were very supportive.

Work was another initiative I buried myself in work.

I was fortunate to have people working for me who were loyal, honest and stuck with me.

Tim was still with me and was determined to do something on his own. I supported that premise and did what I could to help him go out on his own.

He tried hauling oil, hauling logs and nothing paid off.

He ran up some big bills and I came to the rescue every time.

I sold the big hot oiler that Tim was operating and was left with only one that I had rebuilt out of an old abused one I had purchased at Ritchie Brothers in Edmonton. It was Tim and I who had gone up north with these two trucks for one winter to pay bills

Richard Laviolette who had also worked for me in Olds, Wainwright and now Consort was also a huge benefit to Ronwood

There wasn't any truck that Richard couldn't operate. He had a great mechanical knowledge and a stubborn streak.

These Laviolette boys were a big part of Ronwood over the years and I was happy to have had them.

The last hot oil truck I had was the old MACK I had rebuilt from RB Auction.

This one was being operated by Russell Brown from Newfoundland who I had sent money to for the trip out to Consort. Blind trust as all I knew about him was that he had experience running a pressure truck. He sounded sincere and determined so I took the chance and sent him the 2500.00 he figured would get him to Alberta.

He turned up right on time and he proved to be a competent operator and was a barrel of laughs. He and his wife were a welcome addition to Ronwood.

The only other Newfie I had was Don Smith. He was a great salesman and down the road he would prove to be very valuable

The road to success ran through hard work, luck and borrowed money.

We rigged up equipment as needed, diversified to be able to do almost any job in our field of pressure pumping, steam chemical pumping and computer recording of our work.

We went far and wide to build equipment as cheap and as fast as possible. The window of opportunity was not very wide at times.

Financing was far easier to get as there were lease/finance companies willing to take a risk with quicker approval time and a lot less down money to kick it off.

We were fortunate to have the work to pay off past debt. Debt that had been incurred to Sharon's Dad and others who had invested heavily.

We paid all of this debt bond plus the 50,000 Gary Stevens had borrowed from Sharon's Dad, Bill to put into the now defunct razor sharpener business.

We took a lot of pride in paying this all off but for the good fortune of work available this never would have been possible

While Tim was floundering around between hauling oil and hauling logs, Russell Brown who was running the old Hot Oiler I had rebuilt (THE MACK) came up on a corner too fast and rolled the hot oiler. There wasn't too much damage but our insurance company wrote it off as non repairable

They offered 40,000 for payout but I had it insured for 125,000.

The fight was on but they wouldn't change much. I made the deal that they pay me and I would buy back the truck and equipment.

They agreed and I removed the pump, hot oil heater and tank from the MACK truck, sold the truck and pump separately.

I came out ahead this way but I was very disillusioned with the insurance company.

Just after doing all of this Tim and Jody were in trouble financially. I said to Tim why don't you take all of the logging equipment off that nice Kenworth truck and put hot oil equipment on it and do what you know best—'HOT OILING.'

I said "Rig it up and go out west and try the west country again.

We had been there twice before and it was bad timing.

Tim thought that this was a good idea so the wheels were in motion.

The trouble was I had sold the best part off which was the high pressure pump and drive equipment. I called the person and he still had the pump luckily. I paid him an extra thousand to get it back but we had what we needed.

Tim approached John Laan about financing, he went to Fabmaster in Edmonton to get rigged up and soon the truck was rigged and ready.

I helped him get his feet on the ground with operating money and incidentals and away they went to Hinton, AB.

# CHAPTER 53

## Expansion of Trucks and Family

Tim and Jody had a boy and girl as their family. Austin and Alyssa. Healthy, happy and Jody was a great mother. Jody came from a large family and knew what care had to be taken.

Tim was as I was, so wrapped up in work that the kids were not foremost on his mind.

He was aware of their needs and gave them what they needed to the point later of spoiling them with everything they wanted.

Tim was kind and mostly gentle but strict and he expected the best from both.

Jeremy had three all girls. The first was Jordyn. Jordyn was healthy, happy and Krista was the perfect mother as young as she was when Krista gave birth. Krista's mother was a big help because their family was all girls, too.

Jeremy and Krista were living with Sharon and I just before Jordyn was born but then they moved to Krista's parent's place in Compeer.

Jeremy went battery operating for Penn West Petroleum and his days of working for Ronwood were over for a long time.

The second girl was born and was Cerebral Palsy. She was so tiny I couldn't believe it. Just over two pounds from my recollection and the doctor and nurses from Edmonton deserve a great amount of credit for keeping her alive.

They named her Shayna and she became special to everyone. The pain and suffering later proved her to be strong, determined and complaining was not in her vocabulary. As she grew her artistic talents showed her to have writing and art on the horizon.

The third girl was Pyper. She was strong, vibrant and was like a wind up doll that never stopped.

Jeremy was a true father. He was attentive, teaching, firm and they were his first order of duty.

Different from myself and Tim, family came first work second.

As I said earlier Krista is a terrific mother and with a lot of help from mother Joyce and the many aunts who were Krista's sisters.

At this point in time Jennifer our only daughter was still single in university and her family would arrive later.

Sharon loved being a Grandma but with Tim being so far away with his two and Jeremy being amongst his adopted family we didn't see the grandchildren as much as we would have liked to.

When the occasions came Sharon was very happy to be a Grandma.

I was not the "Papa" I wanted to be and I'm sure most of the time the grand kids were afraid of my bark.

I tried but fell short of what I would have liked to show—Love.

These days were busy days for Tim, Jeremy, Sharon and I.

Jeremy would eventually quit his battery operating job and rig up a one ton pressure truck. This put him into the same business as Ronwood and EXTREME HOT OIL which was the name of Tim's new company.

Jeremy named his new company JAG Oilfield Services so we had three companies RONWOOD, XTREME AND JAG.

This was what we wanted, independence from each other and control over our own destiny.

The Alberta way, capitalizing on ambition. Building something out of very little was a proud feeling

We stood up for each other, shared our work if possible and Tim and Jeremy were never bashful about phoning me for advice, parts for the trucks or just to share our experiences good and bad about work

All through the years we needed professional help. We weren't welders or fabricators and if a specialized piece of equipment needed to be built we searched for custom fabricator people who would do what was needed to be done to suit our needs. There were only a few who could do our type of fabrication

One of these in the beginning of Ronwood was Ceda Manufacturing out of Calgary, Alberta. Clint Dyer was the main man behind Ceda and I knew him from Swift Current, Saskatchewan.

He had the look and the build of a bulldog and his determination to get things done made the comparison believable.

Clint and his staff built three trucks for us. One was a rollover accident that surprised everyone and set us back at an extremely busy time.

Clint was building one truck already for us and this one more didn't seem to slow him down. They were building equipment for customers worldwide—India, Russia, China, South America, Mexico and of course the United States.

While I was in Kelowna, B.C. Clint hired me to supervise the building of a hot oiler for India. I did this and this was an experience in itself. I supervised the building, tested the unit and wrote a training manual for them to go by when they got the unit over to India.

This was the last contact I had with Clint Dyer until I moved to Consort from BC. At this time I needed another hot oiler built. This one had to be cheap but with certain specifications that Clint was able to provide. He was however able to put me into contact with a fabricator out of Odessa, Texas by the name of Tommy Southall. Several phone calls later told me that Tommy knew what he was doing. All I had to provide was the truck and a tank to put on the hot oil unit.

No problem. I had the truck and Clint Dyer had an old tank lying in the grass at his acreage.

I loaded the tank, chained it to the frame of the truck and drove to Odessa Texas.

Tommy's company was called Energy Fabrication and they had 12 bays and about 40 men who had many projects such as mine on the go. Most were Mexican origin but I thought they were fantastic.

I travelled to Texas three times to get the truck built. This was a feat in itself as normally 8-10 trips would have to be made.

Tommy had been in the game a long time and his specialty was hot oilers.

I took delivery of this hot oiler on New Year's Eve, arriving at the Canadian Border on New Year's day ready to work. I was met by Sharon, my wife and co owner of Ronwood and Richard Laviolette who would operate this hot oiler. Richard would go on to make a lot of money for us and for himself. I built this truck 55,000 cheaper in the US at that time than it would have cost in Canada. This was a good headstart

In the meantime in Canada we had a fabricating company called Fabmaster out of Edmonton. Ken Foulds was the key man for Fabmaster. Ken and I had many dealings in the past and we got along great.

As things got busier and time to build was critical, prices increased.

I put a lot of faith in Ken as well as any other fabricator and one day I sent a truck to Fabmaster to get a tank inspection. Ken looked at the truck and said go park that piece of junk in the corner. That ended our relationship and business together.

Ken and his staff had done wonderful work building equipment but I was not about to be overcharged or pushed into a corner.

The last fabricator to build for Ronwood was a man by the name of Terry Andersen out of a little town called Lashburn, Saskatchewan.

This happened to come about by chance.

I was in Lloydminster, Saskatchewan looking at trucks on a sales lot when I saw a pressure truck all rigged up for sale.

This is unusual because no one rigs up a truck ready to go to work. I asked the salesman who the fabricating company was that built this truck.

He said "RONERA Manufacturing." "Terry and Linda Andersen own a small fab shop at Lashburn, Saskatchewan."

I soon called Terry and quizzed him on building a pressure truck for RONWOOD.

Terry said "Sure, come on down and we'll talk."

Sharon and I travelled to the acreage (HALF SECTION) that Terry's shop was on. He had all of his welders and equipment compacted into a 3 bay shop close to his house where Linda did all the accounting in an upstairs room.

This to me was amazing in the fact that they produced so much equipment with a few good men. Terry had been welding for many years and he had one foot amputated years before. This didn't seem to impede him, however.

His son Carl and Danny who was his top welder/fabricator and other welders/machinist types that would come and go would do what a lot of high priced shops were doing in the cities.

Terry had a policy that they would only work forty hours per week. This was amazing to me. This was like being in Santa's work shop.

At first I was speculative but after the first truck was built I knew I had made the right decision to get my fabricating work done by them.

Terry has an uncanny ability to envision the end result of whatever he starts without the help of blueprints or computer programs.

There were 2½ hours between our shop and his but that was much better than the trips to Texas and the same distance as Edmonton.

This was around the same time as Pam Huard came to work for Ronwood. She was probably the best addition to Ronwood we had ever had. Aside from being a big help to Sharon with the phones and books, she could do carpentry, yard work, organized the office and she had computer skills.

She and I went on the trips to Lashburn a few times and I knew I hadn't made a mistake by hiring her.

I could pick a good man to hire but a woman was different. She had to be compatible with Sharon and that was not for me to decide. But Sharon and Pam hit it off and for that we were grateful.

Doug Abt, Jaysen Forsberg, Don Smith, Gerald Barber and my son in law Rod Worobo were all hired and fulfilled all that was expected of them.

# CHAPTER 54

# Now I Lay Me Down To Sleep

While we were immersed in work with Ronwood and all of the twists and turns of the business, Jennifer was immersed in studies at the University of Calgary. She was determined to get her degrees and worked hard to get there. Psychology was her aim.

While she went to U of C a fire started which spread to the apartment block she was living in with another girl from the Consort area. They lost everything they had and the loss was devastating to the two young girls. There was no insurance and the communities of Consort, Veteran and Coronation set up fundraising for them. This is the advantage of small communities when there is such a tragedy.

During her time in Calgary Jennifer met up with a friend.

Rod Worobo was his name and they had dated years previous.

They hit it off again and soon were living in Edmonton where Rod got a job as a microbiologist for Maple Leaf Foods. Jennifer was taking part time university courses and working as a travel agent. Life was busy for them and soon two more grandchildren were born. A boy they named Matthew then a girl they named Kylie.

This would be the last of the grandchildren numbering seven, 5 girls and 2 boys. Except for Shayna's affliction with Cerebral Palsy they were all healthy which doesn't say Shayna wasn't happy. She is mastering the way of life she was destined for and surpassing most others with strength and creativeness. A special girl

This should have been the final piece of a complex puzzle with Jennifer and Rod in Edmonton, Jeremy and family in Compeer, Tim and Jody and family in Hinton and finally we would have a good grip on Ronwood.

Soon this was going to unravel as a ball of yarn in a fierce windstorm.

Tim and Jody filed for divorce. There was no way to save this marriage as we as parents found out.

Tim went on to expand his Xtreme Hot oil business and Jody remarried. Both are doing very well so far.

Jeremy stayed with his small business (JAG Oilfield) in Compeer. Family intact

Rod and Jennifer moved to the Okanagan Valley in BC where Jennifer's heart will always be.

This is when Rod decided that he seemed to be losing ground with as much education as he had.

I proposed a deal with Rod and Jennifer to come to work for Ronwood in Consort.

This transpired and the plan was to train Rod as manager.

This was a good plan in the sense that Rod was well trained for management of large businesses. Experience was lacking in the oil business and perhaps I was too impatient.

This was an unfair position for Rod so Jeremy being observant to what was happening suggested that he would manage Ronwood until Rod became more knowledgeable about the business of Ronwood.

This sets the stage and these are the events that preceded the eventual breakdown that would happen to change

1. Steve Piechotta who was my first employee and my nephew was an accident victim while swerving to avoid a deer on the highway ending up as a quadriplegic for life.

2. Sharon's mother (1993) died of cancer in a long painful fight.

3. Sept 6, 2009—Keith Beres who was so close to our hearts and worked for us so many years hit a moose with his Harley Davidson motorcycle and was instantly killed. This was the beginning of this book and the end of an important person to me and many others he was a friend to.

4. July 2010. The loss of my dear sister in law Sheila, wife of my brother Orville. A long terminal illness ended her life. Sheila was an inspiration to my writing and she was attentive to the fact that she knew how to encourage me without changing too much.

5. Sharon's father Bill passed on in Saskatoon Hospital with a blood disease he had for thirty years that should have ended his life in ten years. He had a terrific desire for living and he is terribly missed.

6. The sixth and hardest to take was a good friend, full of ambition and creativity died suddenly on December 23, 1998 of a genetic heart disease she is still highly thought of. A special friend who was the

wife of Clare Cooper who I worked for many hours because he was a consultant and he had faith in our work. He always phoned when he needed our service and we would move things around to accommodate him.

7. Byron Laviolette also passed away October 30, 2010 of a heart attack.

Although he was not part of our business or our lives there was a lot of history in the years gone by and Byron had an impact on our family throughout the years.

As each of these events occurred I felt a loss inside. A loss that was final. There would be no recovering the past only the memories remained. There is no future in dying and I had a difficult time at funerals whether this was a weak belief in an afterlife or spirituality is a guess.

As I got older year by year I felt more vulnerable.

I felt I hadn't achieved anything important in my life.

I couldn't take the best from the past and present to make a better future.

I constantly dwelled on the negative. To me the passing of someone close was negative.

This was a part of a list of excuses to feel sorry for myself. This was part of a bipolar mind primed by alcohol travelling on a one way track of self destructiveness. There is no turning off until there is a wreck. There are no smooth exits.

2011 was a year of ups and downs as usual. This year however had a hurry up side to it.

I knew I was on a manic high and the days had 24 hours to them which I used with very little sleep. Many times I was told I was putting in too many hours working. This was one reason Jeremy offered to help out.

I wouldn't listen to anyone I felt I needed to finish everything at once.

The summer came and went and autumn always creates more work for Ronwood.

Work work work.

The manic high I was on. Instead of reaching out for help I reached for the bottle. A mistake made many times before.

I was lost in the fact I didn't know where to turn.

I turned not to my wife but against her.

I turned not to my family but against them.

I turned not to my work and money but against it.

I turned north in a long white motor home and said good bye to everything.

Now I lay me down to sleep I pray the Lord my soul to keep.

# GALLERY

Carl & Beth Wood
The Wood of Ronwood

Starting Out

Hector and Clara McGregor

Our Youngest Grand Baby

Our Young Family

Matthew
Our Youngest Grand Son

Debbie, Arlene, Doreen, Sharon, Ron, Jack, Gerry and Keith

Bantam Provincial Champions 1990 Jeremy (Jay) behind trophy

left to right Ron, Gerry, Ed, Jack

The Beginning of Skeeter's

Our first hot oil truck 1977

Keith and Ron

My best friend's mother
Kay O'Connor

the six McGregors

Lois, Malcolm, Orville, Vangie, Doreen, Ron

Grand Babies

Jenn's Grad.

Giving Jenn to Rod

Kelowna Shop and Steam Truck

Ruby, Bob Miller, Jim Pagan, Al Lawther, Ron in Center

Ron, Sister Doreen Midge & Glen Hystad

Clare Cooper (Cowboy Hat)

Jim Olson, Ron and brother Orville

1971

Ron and Terry Smart our first drummer who passed away at 43

Sharon, Ron

Five of seven grand children Alyssa, Austin, Pyper, Shayna, and Jordan

Jay, Jenn, Sharon, Tim

Ron, Sharon, Sister Doreen

My nieces
Tracy and Laura Leigh

The crutch I Leaned on
For 39 years Sharon

My Son Jay

My Son Jay

Jack, Dick and Ron practice

Ron and Jack

May they rest in peace
My Dad, Mom Dick and Kay O'Connor

Dick O'Connor just before passing